Blind Vision

VOLUME II

VALUE GIVEN, VALUE RECEIVED

CURTIS C. GRECO

Advantage®

Copyright © 2010, 2011 by Curtis C. Greco

Second Edition.

All rights reserved. No part of this book may be used or reproduced in any manner whatsoever without prior written consent of the author, except as provided by the United States of America copyright law.

Published by Advantage, Charleston, South Carolina.
Member of Advantage Media Group.

ADVANTAGE is a registered trademark and the Advantage colophon is a trademark of Advantage Media Group, Inc.

Printed in the United States of America.

ISBN: 978-1-59932-170-7
LCCN: 2010902355

This publication is designed to provide accurate and authoritative information in regard to the subject matter covered. It is sold with the understanding that the publisher is not engaged in rendering legal, accounting, or other professional services. If legal advice or other expert assistance is required, the services of a competent professional person should be sought.

Most Advantage Media Group titles are available at special quantity discounts for bulk purchases for sales promotions, premiums, fundraising, and educational use. Special versions or book excerpts can also be created to fit specific needs.

For more information, please write: Special Markets, Advantage Media Group, P.O. Box 272, Charleston, SC 29402 or call 1.866.775.1696.

Visit us online at **advantagefamily**.com

"There's an old saying in sports—and elsewhere— that claims rookies get a break because they're 'first-time lucky.' With his first book, We Hold These Truths, *Curtis Greco may have been first-time lucky. With this book,* Value Given, Value Received, *he proves he's second-time brilliant. Greco's new book delivers a winning strategy for America."*

—PAT WILLIAMS, SENIOR VICE PRESIDENT, ORLANDO MAGIC, AUTHOR OF *NAIL IT!* & *DALY WISDOM*

"Curtis Greco wrote a stunning book when he wrote We Hold These Truths. *It was a ringing call to wake up a slumbering nation. Now he's back with* Value Given, Value Received – *and reading it makes me convinced that only vigilance and wakefulness can keep America strong and prosperous."*

—AUSTIN HILL, COLUMNIST, TALK SHOW HOST, AUTHOR OF *THE VIRTUES OF CAPITALISM: A MORAL CASE FOR FREE MARKETS*

"Curtis Greco's second book carries on a grand tradition inherited from the first. Where We Hold These Truths *outlined Greco's vision,* Value Given, Value Received *develops the theme of his work. This is an exciting an innovative approach to political publishing – opinionated, but not partisan. Greco's work stands alongside the best political commentary of the year."*

—TODD ZAUGG, PRINCIPAL & FOUNDER, MATRIX ACHIEVEMENT GROUP, LLC, AUTHOR, *WARRIOR SALES MONK*

DEDICATION:

"...we mutually pledge to each other our Lives,
our Fortunes, and our sacred Honor."

To Carolyn Marie and Jack Ceil; love definitely comes in pairs!

To Americans the world over! This Series is my Gift to you!

But most of all,

To an Infinite and Perfect Love, binding one and all,
from whom "meaning and form" finds its cause!

Blind Vision

NOT SO LONG AGO I had the occasion to sit and visit with my father. At that time, he had progressed well into his 80's and though time had waged a battle with his body, his mind was as crisp as ever. I asked his opinion about the times we are living in and what he observed, over the years, to be the most significant changes. I was amazed by what he said.

- "People, at their core, never really change. However, I have noticed that we seem to have moved away from them [core values]."

- "Despite what history may say, people were not happy about what Roosevelt was doing…it's not all that different from what I see happening today."

- "If there had been the same media exposure of global affairs in the 30's and 40's, Pearl Harbor would never have happened and the American people would have felt much different about the war and Roosevelt would never have been elected."

- "This technology thing – yes, information is more easily obtained, but I think it has pushed people into being more detached and ambivalent."

- "But the thing I've noticed most is that people seem to have lost their sense of common purpose."

If I were to add anything to his comments, I would say the abstract notion of consequence has been degraded and seems to be fading on toward oblivion. We have become desensitized not only to the impact our choices have on our own lives, but perhaps equally important, the impact our choices have on others. This series takes an overview of fiscal interests and policy, not only of the United States, but also of the world, and further examines the financial and social consequences of those very policies. However, I believe the most critical perspective from which to view these issues is through the lens of freedom and the definitive critique of what constitutes the expressions of, or impediments to, liberty.

In one sense, the series may be seen as a *call to action*, in another respect, it may be viewed as a "political and economic retrospective." At best, it may even be both.

To illustrate and underscore this body of work and my own observations and conclusions, I have drawn on a few of my favorite historical figures, such as Thomas Jefferson, Benjamin Franklin, Andrew Jackson, and Don Miguel de Cervantes, to name a few.

A final note on the series title, *Blind Vision*. I appreciate the use of words, in combination, to paint a mental picture from which to convey a message. Let me explain further: Many years ago, I lost an older sister to a congenital heart disorder. Today, modern medicine would likely have saved her; however, it was a different time. Her name was Cynthia – to me though, she was simply known as Cindy. In addition to her heart condition, she was also blind, though she had so well adapted, one would never have known.

As one of 10 children, I am positioned in the younger half of the regiment and occasionally Cindy would be assigned the task of minding a few of the younger group. I was always amazed, no, I was stunned by how she managed to know what sort of trouble I was brewing and her proficiency in interfering with most of my misadventures. I can still, to this very day, clearly hear her voice: "Curtis!"

I recall asking her, "How do you do it?" and she replied, "I'm blind, but I can still see what I know!" Many years would pass and this moment, like others before or since, resolved to memory storage until June of 2008. I had just concluded a talk with a group. A few folks approached me and we began a spirited exchange. As I recall it, I found myself responding to one of the questions with something like this: "Look, even if you were blind, your mind's eye will image what you know to be true!" Instantly, I saw the face of my sister Cindy and I heard her voice once again.

The most compelling reason for this series is my personal love for the ideals that inspired the creation of this country's form of government: "Life, Liberty and the Pursuit of Happiness!" I believe that man's greatest and ultimate challenge is to perfect the means to void his divisive tendencies. Each is called to express ones own unique gift which, in the process of our expressing, defines ones very purpose. However, a gift, by its very nature, can only be expressed in the physical realm and with the rhythm of action, and so, express it we must!

This gift must and will only ever occur freely and with unfettered interchange accompanied by the reward which, I believe, will inevitably come when all engage in the same pursuit. We must move smartly to perfect these ideals and overcome all impediments to its accomplishment. One might even say it is our collective "calling." There is no other place to go; the time is now and the place is right where one finds him or herself to be!

Once I accepted the challenge of actually taking on the project, I found myself wondering if what you are about to read is necessarily new. The manner in which I present the message may be novel and you may even find my own personal comments poetically enticing. However, the fact of the matter is, no matter how well scripted the message may be, we truly do already know the "core values!" I believe God has planted these seeds of truths and they are forever resident in one's mind and soul. They are what you intuitively know to be true.

How then does the idea relate to this three-part series? A fair question. The most efficient way to explain it might best be in the form of an allegory. For instance: A man is walking down the street on his way to work. Summer, winter, rain, snow or shine, year after year, he walks the same course day after day. Some days he gives and some days he receives but always what he carries is a function of what he collects from one place or another. Even without speaking, you know what he does for a living, don't you? Yes, of course you do. The markings are in the images your mind forms from the verbal cues of this simple story. Yes indeed, he's a postman. Simple enough!

Yes, of course the confusion of the day is marked by many indicators of truth sandwiched between the clutter of newspaper articles, five-second sound-bites, talk radio, non-stop breaking news, well crafted speeches and emails. Yet despite the confusion of mixed messages, the markings of what is "true" is found in our conscience which surfaces to filter the input. What we discover from this filtering process is the dissonance between what we observe and what we know, intuitively, to be true. All one is left with is a discordant sense of disbelief which is most conspicuously identified when one finds him or herself uttering: "Who do they think they're kidding?" Well, *they* think it's you!

I, like many, find myself more and more disenfranchised from a political system that bears no resemblance to the promise of our national heritage. Our national sovereignty and economic future has been repackaged and out-sourced with the speed and efficiency of an IRS tax lien; entire industries have been relocated, leaving behind vacant warehouses, silent factories, idle resources of all types and worst of all, broken dreams.

In a country whose very identity rests upon the genius of an ideal that prior to its formation had never seen the light of day, seeing the promise of this land and the industry of so vibrant and genuine a people summarily laid to waste is, as it is for most, simply heart breaking! And then of course are our children, I think of my own and I ask myself: "How can we let this stand?" I hear others say, "What has happened?" I hear even more say, "Somebody's got to do something about this!" And when I hear this comment, I often think of the following story which I heard some years ago. Perhaps one day I'll share the story of how I came to hear it.

It's a story about a man who walks in to a church. You see, he's down on his luck; he's lost his business, he's lost his family and his view of the world is hopeless and in complete disarray. He walks up to the altar and stares squarely at the image upon the cross and with the strained voice of a person in emotional and physical pain he attempts to impale the image with his words. "Why? Why have you done this to me? Why have you let the world fall upon me this way? The world is in turmoil and you sit idly by and just let it happen! What kind of love is this you speak of? How can you speak to me of goodness when this is to be the world in which a man finds himself? Why, oh why, don't you do something?" His energy spent, the room's light gently softens and becomes suddenly still. And then, awakening the stillness of the moment is the warmth of a soft resonant voice and it speaks these simple words: "I did; I sent you."

I'll ask of you this: Please do remember, in particular, the last five words of the preceding paragraph. They are a foundation on which to build a remarkable life!

And so, there it is, the overall message. Read it, enjoy it and be inspired by its message.

BLIND VISION

"I'VE NO NEED FOR VISION TO SEE WHAT I KNOW TO BE TRUE."

CURTIS C. GRECO, JUNE 2009

Contents

A Note from the Author

NOT ENOUGH IS SAID about critical moments in one's life. We often conceal these for various reasons though most often it is more likely that we think, "Oh, we'll get around to it!" or, "Ah, well, I'd better keep it to myself, no one will believe it!" This, however, is not one of those instances. I deliberately intend for all who read these works to know of a specific critical moment and the gratitude I hold in my heart for those who are integral to it. First, the entire staff at Advantage Media Group, an extraordinary group of talented individuals whose assembly is a monument to the truly remarkable vision of Adam Witty, an extraordinary man!

Vision can only ever truly be inspiring if, as its architect, there is an individual capable of its mastery. In Volumes I, II, and III of the *Blind Vision* series, I introduce The Imperfect Messenger Foundation and I fully intend for it to become an iconic resource through which I and others disseminate thought provoking work. And yes, the material you have in hand is indeed the product of my efforts. However, the form you will soon view received its first breath of life from the inspired vision of Denis Boyles, AMG's Senior Editor to whom I will be eternally grateful! For me, mastery is only ever known when combined with action: Editor Priscilla Turner is the archetypical form of this ideal and has demonstrated it so lovingly through her guidance, precision and elegant refinements. From where I started, even I could never have imagined the result and I will look forward to working with her again and again.

To say that I have saved the *best for last* would not be fair to those I've mentioned thus far, so perhaps it is more appropriate for me to express my intention this way: I've saved the most dear for last! Gregg Stebben is an exceptionally gifted gentlemen. I've known him since I was 15 years old and although we accompanied events and careers which led us on separate paths for much of this time, a wondrous fate brought us back together. For this, I've only to express a hearty thanks to his marvelous brother, Marty. To the point: It is not an overstatement to say that none of what is before you would appear the way it does were it not for Gregg. He possesses a unique self-effacing form of warmth and gentleness that is supremely magnetic. He is an accomplished writer and media presence and most importantly, he is truly a good man in every sense of the word. I do my best to express regard and admiration for him at every possible opportunity.

And so you ask: *What is the critical moment?* Consider, if you will, thinking of life as a canvas upon which each of us records and expresses our own unique and individual gift in a color and by a stroke uniquely our own. Not one stroke may be omitted, not one expression missed or unrecorded — to do so would forever change the image and then for all time it would remain incomplete. For me, the *critical moment* for this endeavor is this: That at one moment in time I should be so blessed to have such magnificent talent expressing their gift upon my canvas! To omit just one would have made the outcome something different, something less! They have given me an extraordinary gift which I now present to you the Reader and I do believe we owe each other our very best effort. I couldn't possibly imagine a more perfect way to paint a life in color!

A Perspective

I TRUST YOU HAVE READ Volume I of the series: *We Hold These Truths.* If you have not, may I suggest that you do as what follows in this, Volume II, is a critical extension of the very fundamentals presented throughout the opening *volume* and each are integral not only to our idea of what freedom is but also its natural extension, your personal industry.

I am very passionate about the subject of what I refer to as *kinetic behavioral dynamics (KBD)* and it is a subject I thoroughly enjoy presenting to a willing audience. As is the case with finance and economics, both an extension of one's *personal industry, KBD* is nothing more than the integration of the human force and the consequential, i.e., *cause* and *affect* (yes, I mean *affect*), which lies behind all human *motive* force and how we (humans) orient ourselves to address individual life experiences. This notion, *KBD*, developed from my personal exploration of the motive force that *inspires action* and my companion inquiry into the thoughts and commentaries of Emmet Fox (whose writings I highly recommend). Understanding and integrating his teachings served me well in refining the entire *KBD* concept primarily due to the inspired simplicity of one of his most notable expressions:

> *"The Science of Living is the Science*
> *of Mastering your thinking!"*

It is to this specific point of his comment, that is, how one *thinks* about a certain issue or event – that I find critical to how one orients himself to the concepts we will consider throughout the chapters that follow. As I often say: *what you think becomes what you know and how you think about what you know resolves in what you do*!

How we orient our thoughts and actions to the environment we find ourselves in is directly related to how we comprehend or perceive our relationship to it. In the section on *Monetary Policy* I introduce a conceptual notion that I refer to as *shades of gray*; when you happen upon this section the concept of *relationship,* referenced previously, will become clearer. I hope to make the point that what might otherwise appear to be a dreadfully boring subject (*economics and money*) is actually an intensely relevant and personal issue, though I readily admit it may not seem so at first glance. Take comfort in knowing in advance that what you are about to read is in no way an academic or an exhaustive exercise in the near infinite permutations of *economics and finance;* it is, as I intend, an intensely individual philosophical discussion.

To be sure, this particular subject is inseparable from the human experience for the simple reason that it is both perfectly aligned with your *inalienable rights* and a direct link to the expression of your innate genius and divinity, the likes of which is expressed nowhere else and in quite the same way as in you, the individual.

The Creator may very well have replicated and/or partitioned a portion of his life force so as to fuel the human *being,* but in this, perhaps his only single uniform human application, he also set about the intricate task of what may best be characterized as a uniquely supreme individual expression of infinite potential – *You!*

For this reason I believe the arrangement of this material, as it appears in each of the three *volumes,* is so strategically relevant. I am of the opinion, taken from the aggregation of my studies and personal experiences, that the last 100 years of American history illustrates the progressive acceleration of our individual degradation, the cause of which is directly related to the abuses of the political, economic and monetary components of the American expression! It has been and continues to be a seemingly impenetrable structure whose form, I promise, only seems to be formidable. In fact, as an affirming reference, one only has to bear witness to the fracturing of its organisms to observe its systemic weaknesses and vulnerabilities.

As we are each individuals going about our days and making our way through the various tasks at hand, we experience the hardships of these abuses and we see the scars on the faces of our fellow Americans each of which mark our collective course. But to be frank, I am not so much concerned for those who may never be willing to take up the challenge of expressing and bringing to physical form the beneficial reward and product of their divinely inspired genius. No, to be sure, the unwilling will always be a part of mankind. I am, however, gravely concerned for the *willing* who go about their day engaged in the seemingly endless endeavor toward perfecting the mastery of their own unique and divinely-inspired form. Not only does mankind, particularly the aged and infirmed, rely upon the industry of these individuals, they are also an inspiring necessity for us all! These people represent the lifeblood and kinetic source of all divinely inspired action the likes of which have propelled mankind from his lesser origins.

However this kinetic force, apparently, is still not enough. We have more to do and more to perfect in the doing! The task will require not a village of the mindless but instead, a legion of individuals willing to arouse, intuitively, what is most righteous at their core converging upon an inspired ideal. For me, I *Stand 4*[1] this occurring and for those of you who are among the willing, I will be honored to stand with *you!*

I am reminded of a story I heard some years ago, and perhaps this is an appropriate time to share it with *you!*

A man and his wife were walking along the shore, the sand resonating its warmth through the skin of their bare feet. The sky was a magnificent sight complete with the occasional tuffs of white clouds lingering about – a few gently kissing the horizon – the sea, tranquil and a pearlescent azure-blue. As they walked along the water's edge they noticed in the distance, a man walking toward them who appeared to persistently reach down, pick something up and toss it in to the sea.

As the couples' distance between this man and their position closed, they realized they were standing in a field of starfish which the storm surge, from the night before, had left stranded upon the shore. They approached him and said, "We were wondering what you were throwing into the ocean!"

The man replied, "Yes, look at them, thousands of star fish stranded on the beach; isn't it amazing? I'm throwing them back!"

---

1 *Stand 4* is a proprietary expression of mine used in other applications. This expression is used to highlight the kinetic force one must first identify and comprehend in order to know what it means to *Stand 4* some *thing* but more importantly, to grasp the compelling reasons for why a *thing* needs to be *Stood 4* in the first place. One might express it this way: I *Stand 4* Freedom as it is worth *Standing 4* and it is my intuitive sense of Grace, Fidelity, Honor and Commitment to a Fundamental Adherence of Providential Ideals which defines my character and thus, fuels ones compulsion to *Stand 4* a thing in the first place.

"Oh!" the couple replied in a rather perplexed tone, "But there are so many of them; how can you possibly make a difference?"

The man looked down, picked up another starfish and threw it back in to the sea and said, "Made a difference to that one!"

And so, as you read and ponder the chapters that follow, I encourage you to consider the material not as a maze from which to overwhelm the system of your senses, but as a component of a much greater cause whose cure, one by one acting in unison, will make a difference even if only for the *One!*

And so, once again, on behalf of myself, its author, and

THE IMPERFECT MESSENGER FOUNDATION

I present to you:

BLIND VISION
VOLUME II
VALUE GIVEN, VALUE RECEIVED

Enjoy!

CURTIS C. GRECO

Value Given, Value Received
Simple Economics

"I'VE NO NEED FOR VISION TO SEE WHAT I KNOW TO BE TRUE."

LIKE MANY MEMBERS of the proletariat, I too enjoy tinkering with all things mechanical. I enjoy, in particular, power tools and I possess a handsome collection of all types. I marvel at the mind of a person who can conceive and design as well as a system that can assemble the means to manufacture these wonderful time and labor saving devices.

In its most basic form, the aforementioned is the gestating *economic engine;* observing a need and articulating the means necessary to fill it. In its more complex form it can also be observed in the evolution of technological innovations creating the potential for *demands* that heretofore no one knew or ever thought would exist; for example, a cellular telephone!

The process of identifying and meeting *demand* expressed by or within a progressive cycle, achieved through the exchange of means and resources between and amongst the participants of this very process is *simple economics.*

Again, as was the case with Volume I and the review of our Constitutional structure, I have no intention of creating a self-study course in economic theory, however, I do believe it is necessary to bring to the discussion a few economic principles that, frankly, are largely ignored in contemporary discourse. Whatever the depth of discussion a reader of this work might claim should have been explored is only to prove the following point: When enduring the crisis of converging intentions, *it is all too often the case that it is the obvious that is least visible.*

Yes, by all means, we might engage in extended discussions on *micro* and *macro-economics;* I could create a treatise on various economic *theories,* among these Keynesian, Marxist, classical, neo-classical, Milton Friedman's, etc., but that would be to no productive purpose. Rather, I intend to address economics at its most robust and fundamental core. It is from this *root causes* that we might determine *why* these fundamentals are so important if for no other reason than to grasp how reliance on *theory* is so very dangerous.

I issue the reader a *warning* in advance! If you found offense and/ or disagreement with *Volume I: We Hold These Truths,* then you must know I'll continue to fuel your displeasure. Every position advanced in the following is an extension of thought whose ultimate resources are the fundamental principles upon which this country was founded. End of story. Onward!

As many great discoveries have their origins, so did my own process of economic maturation. I'm reminded of my college years and one particular graduate-level course. The class was mandatory and as I recall it possessed the creatively inspired title, "Advanced Economic Theory." I admit I was not the best student, the root cause of which, as best I can explain, was that I seemed to struggle with the abstractions of theory and its relevance to the practical. Case in point: Integral to one's success in the program was the authoring of a *paper,* a thesis of sort. I mined my brain for a time and came up with what I thought to be an inspired topic, which, for various reasons, was to ultimately prove my undoing (at least as far as the class was concerned.) The topic can be best characterized as *A Study in the Practical Applications of Economic Theory.*

At this point in my career I was doubling as a student and working full time in the public accounting profession and I was resigned to the conclusion that my undergraduate curriculum inadequately prepared me for the practical demands of the profession. Now then if that weren't sufficient to occupy my time, I now had to deliver, on command, my work product to a suede-elbow-patched tweed-wearing tenured professor, who, as it turns out, possessed no practical economic experience *what so ever* and I was in no way or form pleased with the whole idea. To be sure I struggled greatly with the project, primarily as I ultimately realized that the fundamental concepts I was working with were, to me, painfully incongruent! These *concepts* being, of course, *practical* and *theoretical!* In the end, yes, I did complete the paper, which was summarily dismissed with what I later would muse as comments that were strangely incongruent as well. I've no idea what happened to the paper; it is likely that I burned it in protest. However, the critique has permanently stained my collegiate memory: "...woefully pagan and self-indulgent, yet practical conclusion..." I still have no idea what this means!

A few years passed and I'd migrated to the real estate profession during the time of the *Savings and Loan crisis.* I was working on liquidating portfolio assets of various *institutions* that had been placed under the control of the Resolution Trust Corporation (RTC). It was during this phase in my career that a symposium had been scheduled and was slated to be led by a panel of representatives from various government agencies, one professor of economics and a few representatives of the banking and real estate industries. As I recall, the event was a two-day long forum; a banal form of torture and I was required to be in attendance. It was during the last of a series of *breaks* that I was pulled by a fellow broker into a group of attendees who were quizzing one of the government's experts. It wasn't long before he leaned into my ear and said, "What d'you think about all this?" I thought for a moment and juckled, recalling my paper and said, *"Theoretical makes great conversation, but incongruent with results when in practice! The limitations of government are never more apparent than in the case of legislation-enacted chaos. It seems strange to me to have the very same individuals who lacked any degree of constructive intellect and foresight when crafting the legislation be the very same ones who are engaged in repairing its damage! Government never corrects its mistakes, it simply passes new legislation in an attempt to mask another!"*

In the economic conundrum of the late 1990's many of the same issues that ignited the firestorm of the RTC days surfaced once again. On this occasion however, it was me who was called upon to make a comment on economic issues specifically as it related to the real estate industry. In preparing for my presentation I quickly came to the realization that to be fair to the discussion I had to consider the economic issues in a far greater scope than simply from an industry-specific and regional perspective. I had the basics down in the form of an outline however, in order to provide continuity on the subject I needed to establish a foundation for my commentaries. I required a point of reference; what I needed was a *model* that was functional and easy to understand.

The component result of this personal inquiry was required of me to revisit a subject from several years earlier. Yes, it was my "…woefully pagan and self-indulgent, yet practical conclusion" that was going to be my messenger! To be quite honest, I've used it several times since to explain the seemingly unexplainable and I've come to be quite proud of its rather "pagan and self-indulgent" observations but even more, its simplicity. In this forum, particularly in the current economic environment, it is this very simplicity that I believe to be a very effective compass in our effort to set us straight. I trust I've piqued your curiosity!

As I considered it then and came to realize that I still do, this *functional economic model*[2] is marvelously effective, primarily because it is so simple. It is best defined by the following two fundamental concepts: *wealth creation* and *wealth consumption*. The extent to which an economy is functionally vibrant is the extent to which *wealth creation* exceeds *wealth consumption*. The extent to which an economy is functionally flaccid or dying is the extent to which *wealth consumption* exceeds *wealth creation*. This model also presumes that the only defining means of *wealth creation* resided solely in *productive capacity*, be it consumer, industrial, productive industry,[3] raw material, farming or intellectual/innovative (but only to the extent the intellectual/innovative productivity migrated and became manifested in the former). In other words, using an example of technological innovation; the personal computer, the VCR/DVD, etc., may very well find its conception by way of domestic creativity; however, in effect, if the product (finished) as conceived is manufactured through sources beyond the domestic shore there is little, if any, beneficial economic effect as to the principle of *wealth creation* for an economic sphere, i.e., a nation or economic unit. In truth, this version or type of *off-shoring* is a pre-

---

2   Nearly every component of what is discussed in Volumes I, II, and III is an extension of this model.

3   Productive industry was my way of defining the "industrial capacity industry." It is industrial capacity that produces the instruments/hardware/means of production. In other words, you may want to manufacture automobiles, however, an economy must first possess the ability to manufacture the tools, the machinery, the assembly lines, etc., in order to engage in the production of automobiles.

dictably malignant form of *wealth consumption* far beyond what most realize. More on this point in short order.

In this *model* one might find it interesting that *wealth consumption* concludes that any item not a component of the *wealth creation* engine is then a *consumer of wealth,* notable among these being: government spending (in all forms) as well as nearly all *service-based* expenditures. Needless to say, I disagree with the notion that the U.S. economy can be a *service-based economy* and yet still be considered economically viable. Again, as mentioned previously, this model easily demonstrates *services* as being a consumer of wealth and we will discuss the point further and in due course.

In a *service based economy,* as there is no *wealth creation,* spending can only be subsidized by *debt creation.* Observing the last 45 years of American economic history alone, if one were only to consider consumer debt (ignoring the explosion of federal and state government deficit/debt-funded spending), indicates just how accurate the model/observation is. Further, I suggested that investment, strange as it may seem, is somewhat of a neutral component of *wealth consumption* unless it is component-investment toward productive capacity. I proffered then as I do now that it (investment) is an *indicator* of *economic momentum.* The product of thought being that there was a correlation between how much an economy expended in self-perpetuation, i.e., productivity investment and in the instances as a negative indicator, such as speculative investment, that it did not. A few remnant thoughts relating to the *model,* are as follows:

1. The model was a *snapshot* ambition intended to give only a current indicator and *marker* for *short-term measure* and *trending* for long term outlook.

2. It holds that due to the nature of *demand* and *business cycles,* over the horizon trend analyses were merely prognostications. Further, the model assumes an *adaptable* economic infrastructure that, due to the nature of *adaptive* and *native* tendencies is, at best, a 24 to 36 month cycle, though more often far more narrow in span and precisely why an economy needs to be *adaptable.*

3. The *model* maintains that the *service sector,* like government, is a *consumer of wealth* for the following reasons: (i) The service function is merely transference of *wealth* and produces no effective/ tangible economic yield. And, (ii) The transference of wealth is/ becomes a taxable event that, in effect, perpetually diminishes the incremental value which ultimately exhausts the dollar unit transferred in a *service* based transaction.

4. The economic *model* views government intervention, within the domains of its mandate, as non-adversarial.

5. The ideal of corporate responsibility is equivalent, or on par with individual responsibility. More specifically, there is economic value in good-faith practices.

6. Monetary policy should be an extension of *wealth creation* and views *debt creation* as a *consumer of wealth,* particularly government debt accumulation as it diverts financial resources away from the productive *wealth creation* cycle. The idea holds that as with private enterprise, government should be financially self-reliant[4] and not parasitic.

7. It views economic vitality as a *bottom up* source identifier, not as a *top down* motive.

---

4   Revenues generated from the economic cycle only. Views individual and corporate income tax as a *wealth consumer,* which diverts post-productive resources from reinvigorating the *wealth creation engine,* which, in reality, is precisely what occurs.

8. The model as a core intention, never considers that the process functions as intended, only that it will continuously refine until it does. If not, it will self-defeat and be replaced with a more efficient mechanism. Capitalism intuitively moves to perfect the process as a fundamental *life-sustaining source*. I refer to this *fundamental life source* as the *native economy*. In other words, the system is *self-correcting* and this observation will be intuitively understood by any individual who operates a business for profit.

To be sure, this presentation (above) is most certainly neither arcane nor ground-breaking in scope. Yes, were I to fully develop the concepts therein, we might yet conclude a rather exhaustive study of its true potential and identify the few, if any, consequent limitations. Perhaps we'll leave this as a project for another time. However I believe it important to set forth what has been an observation my inquiry made abundantly clear which is this: Economic theory is only theory! It may set forth topics that give a name to what is observed in an economic system but is far from being an effective tool from which to determine a manipulated or prescribed outcome. The infinite possibilities of unintended outcome are simply far too diverse to measure making the results tentative at best or simply unreliable. Any individual or enterprise that functions within the realm of productive outcome, which of course excludes government, understands that at the end of the month, if you've paid all of your bills and you have money left, then you've made a profit. Conversely, unless of course you are a government entity or non-profit, at the conclusion of your *business cycle* should your *wealth consumption* exceed your *wealth creation,* you've sustained a loss. Simplicity is a principle the convoluted need to become acquainted with!

Still, from the "macro" perspective the *model* also works surprisingly well. When the U.S. economic engine was at its peak (1947 through the later part of the 1960's), it illustrated the efficiency of this model quite well. Peculiar as it may seem, the idea models the U.S. economy *in decline* as well.

Before moving on, there is one specific issue I've discovered that bears mentioning as I find that it yields a clarifying effect. The clarification is, first and foremost, present by understanding the scope of what an economic system can do and what it cannot. It is simply, at its best and most efficient, *only* a point of departure. As in the case of the foundations on which the United States is based, once the beneficial mechanism is in place, what is done with it is up to you! The economic engine, when practiced in a free and just society, is a *remarkably productive and robust enterprise*. It is equally important to consider the idea of *potential* when evaluating what this system does; it will not, alas, inspire the unwilling! Of course it is no small mention to consider as well that the economic engines' robustness is driven only by a previously mentioned concept, the *native economy*. Despite what the politician might like you to believe, it is *not* driven by government *stimulus*. In point of fact, the economy's durability is burdened, in a multiplying affect, by this very type of meddling.

"FUNCTION PERSISTS ONLY SO LONG AS FORM IS ITS PERSISTENT COMPANION. THE DISTORTION OF ONE INVARIABLE DEFEATS THE OTHER! IN THIS, THERE ARE NO EXCEPTIONS."

How the rewards of this productive engine are applied should never be the domain of *any* entity other than those whose efforts fuel that very engine. For the time being I will leave this simply as an abstract notion; rest assured though, the reader will clearly grasp the substantive value as we observe the frequency of its occurrence. These violations are easily measured from the effects of intrusive government as well as the reckless trade practices that have given rise to the canard known as globalism. For now, just consider this principle as an extension of the various points discussed in *Volume I: Selective Ideals,* and throughout the remaining discussion of this *volume* and *Volume III: Valor in Prosperity.*

In short form, I believe that if you've earned it, it is your property. If it is your property, it is also yours to do with as you please! "Thou canst not…" claim property that is not yours simply by the act of *taking.* Now, on the other hand, if one sees a benefit in exchanging your industry (or product of the same) for consideration in any form you choose to accept then that too, is your choice and yours *alone.*

These views, when seen as those of a simpleton, will likely attract the contempt of a sophisticate who will equip himself with all manner of wildly creative examples of their limitations. This erudite species will say, "But what of the role of government?" or "How will the system protect the people against the abuses of the wealthy?" not to the exclusion of other self-propogating intonations; an absolute certainty. You know these life-forms; they're the *collectivists.* Well, I will address these as well, shortly. Before doing so, I'd be remiss were I not to discuss monetary policy in a more complete context. It is an extremely important subject and I want to assure the readership that I will address it in a later chapter.

ADAPTABLE AND SELF-RELIANT

In an era of the construct that has become the *global economy,* I believe we need to devote to the subject a measured degree of attention. Consider: *Monetary policy* is no longer simply the administration and the methodical guardianship of a nation's financial resources and the medium (currency) by which it is exchanged. No, it has become it own entity! Suffice it to say, it is relevant to the discussion, not only as it relates to where we've been and where we are, but also the methods we might employ to affect what I will simply, for now, refer to as our *economic reinvention*! We will explore this concept fully in *Volume III.* With this aside, at least temporarily, let us continue on!

For some strange reason I have long enjoyed the subject of political and economic history. A component observation of the interaction of *individual interests* and the interchange of *economic motives* is that they are most often contaminated by the device of *political influence.* In *Volume III: Valor in Prosperity,* I will present the idea that freedom and the extent to which it is in play is, largely, a function of the conviction of *The People's* willingness to preserve it. Though consider the following if you will: Is this not the case in every facet of human existence? Who among us can separate the ideals which are concomitant with architecture of *providential design* from the qualitative value of the human experience? They are, pointedly, inseparable for as we converge upon these ideals of perfection we experience the beneficial rewards. Conversely, as we move further away, we endure the expanse in the company of adverse consequence.

"THE GREATER ERROR OF GOVERNMENT IS THE PRESUMPTION
THAT LEGISLATIVE ACTION SOMEHOW VOIDS PREDICTABLE
CONSEQUENCE; THE PRETENSE OF MAKING LEGAL AN ACTION
THAT CLEARLY TRANSGRESSES INVIOLABLE LAW AND THUS
HAVING DONE SO BELIEVED TO BE INCONSEQUENTIAL, IS
BUT AN OPEN INVITATION TO PUNITIVE INEVITABILITY!"

The following point is yet another observation that I believe worth integrating in to the discussion; I might even go so far as to suggest that you read it multiple times so as to be sure to fully blend its message into your notional composition of this topic:

"IN THE PRESERVING OF FREEDOM WE ACCOMPANY FIRST
HAND THE FINEST DEMONSTRATIONS OF ITS FUNDAMENTAL
PRINCIPLES. HOWEVER, WHEN FULLY ENGAGED WITH THE
COMPANIONSHIP AND SIMULTANEOUS STROKE OF INSPIRED
ACTION, WE WITNESS THE PERFECT EXPRESSION OF ITS VALOR!"

An extension of this principle is the concept of *self-reliance.* In its most fundamental terms we might even say that the degree to *which a people are prosperous is directly related to the degree to which they are free. Free* to engage in the unfettered exchange of their goods and services for those of another. When one is at liberty to express their personal industry unobstructed by the divisiveness of government intervention, they simultaneous define and demonstrate the very meaning of *freedom* and its dynamic multiplier, *self-reliance.*

The practical application of *simple economics,* as defined above in terms of the *functional economic model,* is brought to life in the domain of a *self-reliant people,* pure and simple. Do not be intoxicated with the simplicity of this seemingly anecdotal illustration; make no mistake, it is the very underpinnings of the American economic success story. It is, in fact, the iconic *for-profit model*. The basic and fundamental desire of man to be, do and have better! *This is, in practice, the heart (the pulse) of the native economy and so grotesquely misunderstood!* Whatever excesses or lawlessness it may have generated, which could easily have been cured by existing law and/or through judicial means, was and has always been made worse by the biased ambitions of misguided government intervention.

A vibrant and adaptable economic system creates wealth proportionate to the strength of its motive force. As we've seen in American economic history, this motive force has been profoundly efficient. It has fueled economic advancement the benefits of which have been dispersed the world over. The question of whether it works should, once and for all, be put to an end. Suffice it to say, it does (function quite well), but again only *to the extent it is permitted!* It has spawned economic growth and technological advancements to such a degree that the system was sufficiently productive to pull the world out of starvation, economic depression, tyrannical lapses in judgment *(world wars)* and through the later part of the 1960's, with sufficient motive force to tolerate and fund, initially, explosive growth in government spending!

"THE ECONOMIC POWERHOUSE OF THE AMERICAN
ECONOMIC SYSTEM IS NOT SIMPLY CAPITALISM; IT IS THE
EXPRESSION OF AN INSTINCTIVE AND COMPELLING URGE
MASTERFULLY PRACTICED WHEN IN THE HANDS OF A FREE
PEOPLE OPERATING IN A JUST SOCIAL ENVIRONMENT."

It is important to remember that this ALL happened not because of government, but in spite of it! The overwhelming preponderance of historical evidence is incontrovertible.

An economic system, such as that which existed in the U.S., is a highly charged environment. It operates in response to the most powerful form of compulsion which by its nature is inconspicuous and for this reason, nearly impossible to measure, yet its effects are clearly visible. It is the reason a demand exists and also the reason demand changes so abruptly. It is the origin of impulse and the arbiter of aversion. It is also an integral component of the system's ability to adapt, to adjust and to reset itself. This form, the source of compulsion, is none other than man himself. It is a core quality; we are a creator of constant thought and constant state of action whether physical or mental. *Even asleep, we are not at rest.* Likewise, it is perfectly understandable that an extension of this motive force, when left to its most creative and inherent self-expressive nature, will produce a *thing* that bears the mark of its very creator. Like begets like, does it not?

By way of affirming both the previous and the following paragraph, I trust you'll enjoy the subtitles of a simply wonderful quatrain. It belongs to the splendored genius of Omar Khayyam's *Rubaiyat:*[5]

> *"For in the Market-place, one Dusk of Day,*
> *I watch'd the Potter thumping his wet Clay:*
> *And with its all obliterated Tongue It murmur'd*
> *'Gently, Brother, gently, pray!'"*

---

5   Omar Khayyám (1048–1131), a Persian poet, mathematician and astronomer.

Yes, even the "wet clay" hopes for the fullest possible expression at the hand of man's divinely inspired genius. To be sure, Nature's forms are compelled by their own uniquely prescribed intentions.

Owing then to its nature, the American economic system, when tampered with, can and does run afoul. In the final volume of the series, *Volume III: Valor in Prosperity*, we discuss more fully many of these issues and in what way the system may attempt to restore balance, however for now, let us review basics of the *System-Operational Parameters*:

1. The system will produce no more than the sum of its input.

2. The system creates no wealth beyond the tangible value it generates.

3. There is a law of economic balance that enables the system to function. And,

4. The *law* then proves its features by observing that any imbalance or perversion of either #1 or #2 fouls #3.

If you doubt the validity of these operational parameters (OP's) consider the following: The *system* identifies a need to hydrate four individuals setting out on foot for a five-day hike in the Sierra Nevada range. It is determined that the potential demand for water requires one gallon per day per person for a total of 20 gallons of water. Price and terms are agreed to and the system adapts to the demands of the venture and facilitates the production by making available the requisite supply of bottled water. Couldn't be more simple. Now then, let us add a bit of *government intervention* to the mix of our four tourists – an additional four unexpected guests – and observe what happens to the status quo. Yes, one could simply ration the water and give each the same number of (partial) glasses per day[6]. However, and notwithstanding your most imaginative and specious assurances, you'll never be able to deliver on the promise of one gallon per day, per person!

The notion of taking a sum from one and giving it to another may sound egalitarian but the idea is strictly dysfunctional in practical terms. In truth, it is not the system that is broken as it met the prescribed requirements fabulously but simply that the random imposition is not what the system is structured to address; which, by the way, is not the same as what the system *can* produce. To be more precise: It should not be presumed that the system is unable to meet the additional demand, as this is a wholly separate issue and never *even* considered. It is, however, that the system is being asked to fulfill or accommodate a demand that is greater than the sum-total of the resource provided. In other words, from our previous example, the *system* is being asked to produce 40 gallons of water from a source of only 20 gallons. This is the illusion of the *collectivist* who espouses big government (and also the very same apocryphal design of our monetary/banking system) who either doesn't *get it* or simply doesn't want to.   He only knows the idea of rendering unto him that which is yours and expecting you to provide it!

"THERE IS NO LIMITATION ON SUPPLY; THERE IS
ONLY LIMITATION IN THOUGHT AND THE EFFORT
REQUIRED TO BRING ITS REWARD TO LIFE!"

Yes, of course it is a seemingly simplistic illustration, and deliberately so. Nonetheless, it illustrates several points that are either conveniently

---

6   This would be the ideal opportunity for the *Financial Markets* to churn the cream. Whereas and not unlike their faux-market for Mortgage Instruments, they would create a series of *instruments* (derivatives) that would trade based on the market value of the non-existent "20 Gallons" and the other being a *security* that represents the risk of one of the eight dying from dehydration.

ignored or deliberately overlooked – *what an economy can do and what it cannot.* It also validates the four System Operational Parameters, presented above and as follows: (a) The system will only produce the number of bottles (by volume) equal to the number of gallons of water placed in the system in the manner and form prescribed (Rule #1). (b) The rewarding effects of the water will only *ever* be to the extent hydration benefits the hiker (Rule #2). By the way, how the hiker uses or applies the benefits of being hydrated is left to his discretion. (c) The system fulfilled its contractual obligations by providing the bottled water as specified and received just payment as consideration for its efforts (Rule #3). And, (d) The moment the system's performance (its degree of success) was measured against a subsequent demand, i.e., the addition of four guests, the expectations and outcome became incompatible with the structure of its mandate (Rule #4) and thus, it predictably fails.

In other words, *whatever wealth is created becomes a measured quantity; partitioning in whatever degree you may choose or among as many people as you like does not increase its value.* In fact what happens, as we see in the example above, the effort simply diminishes the unit value of the water (deflation) and simultaneously fabricates a false demand (inflation) – not unlike what occurs in the real estate market cycles. In the case of the hikers, *it's not that they live longer; they just die a little slower!*

This example, in effect, presents the illusion of *collectivist economic ideology* which begets the toxic fuel that *kills a vibrant economic system.* To be sure, they can feed the masses and concurrently ignore the fact that their growing burden is producing an ever-diminishing supply of food. We'd do well to remind ourselves of the former Soviet Union's economic system particularly if (as some may) my anecdotal commentary is considered as being without basis in fact.

Here are two additional examples where Rule # 4's consequential effects are triggered:

1. Any effort by the government to stimulate the economic system or cycle through regulation, arbitrary predation, monetary accretion and/or wealth consuming entitlement burden. Example: Government spending programs that provide no economic benefit, such as social welfare programs or price support systems/subsidies.

2. Extracting value out of the system by placing demands that are not congruent with its functional mandate. Examples: Progressive tax strategies that have multiple tax burdens on *distributed income* which are predictably prohibitive as to savings, investment and productive expansion. Predatory *collective bargaining* practices that *consume* in excess of their productive contribution. Systemic government *deficit spending* and dominance in *gross domestic product* (GDP) composition, which, at the present time greatly exceeds the total *wealth creation* output of the nation. And finally, destructive trade policies that have summarily dismantled the *wealth creation* capacity of the nation.

Before moving on let us review a few remaining points which I trust will encapsulate the functional purpose of the current discussion and, as was the intention, the preceding illustration. Consider, if you will, the following points:

*   An *economic system* can and will only produce wealth to the extent that the system is fueled sufficiently to create it.

- *Wealth creation* does not, nor will it ever, occur in a vacuum or absent the necessary means.

- So called *financial markets,* in the absence of wealth creation, do not generate liquidity, they only *create* the appearance of capital flow through fabricating markets which consist (only) of churning fiat instruments of value. Not unlike government, there economic gain occurs only from what the extract from the churning process occurring in their system, i.e., the *financial markets.*

- The government *means,* or resources, no matter the mandate, no matter the bilious cooing of your favorite politician or the burden they may place or assert upon the economic system, will never positively affect the *wealth creation cycle, ever!*

- There are two and *only* two ways the economic system *adapts* to government impositions: It slowly dies from exhaustion or it moves on to a more accommodating environment[7] leaving the empty shell of the once vibrant form to the memory of what once was.

> "THERE IS NO WEALTH CREATED IN RECALLING PAST
> SUCCESS. THERE IS ONLY LAMENTING THE IMPLIED
> FAILURE WHICH ACCOMPANIES THEIR ABSENCE!"

In *Volume I,* the section entitled *The Policy of Economic Conflict and Selective Ideals,* I presented several examples of the adaptive form of government. If you, the reader, have not yet read the rich treatise

---

7   Environment, in this instance, does not necessarily mean that it relocates. It can also mean that the system *morphs* into another form. It can become predatory, such as in the case of *globalism*, which is the most intrusive and the most visible.

on this subject, I heartily recommend obtaining a copy for your permanent library. For the time being though, do give ample thought to the following:

Believing that government can modify the system to suit its ambition is to believe, serendipitously, that the *law of economic balance* does not universally apply (which it does). Holding to this belief simply provides, as a matter of certainty, government license to habitually violate this law and insure its enduring imposition and the lasting consequences of having provided both accommodations. *In this instance, as we see in our time, the system is effectively left to feed upon itself by holding to the belief that an ever-evolving form of government entitlement ascends to and position itself as a rightful and most righteous arbiter of economic success!*

> "AND THEN, SOMETHING THAT ONCE WAS, ONCE ALTERED, HAS NOW BECOME SOMETHING ELSE!"

I can think of few references that better underscore the rudimentary elements of *precision economic* and *monetary policy* than the following:

> *"Let honesty and industry be thy constant companions, and spend one penny less than thy clear gains; then shall thy pocket begin to thrive; creditors will not insult, nor want oppress, nor hungerness bite, nor nakedness freeze thee."* [8]

Mr. Franklin, as evidenced by his own words, understood the relationship of *wealth creation* to *wealth consumption* quite well. His statement illustrates that *spending* is not the same thing as *wealth creation* but only a *potential component* of an economically vibrant system: "Spend one penny less than thy clear gains." His words were deliberate and acutely intuitive. Depending on one's priority as to the function of *spending*, the outcome could be at either end of the spectrum, i.e., *productive* or *consumptive*. In either case he understood that whatever the outcome, the functional efficiency of the system was not the issue *but merely to be viewed as a tool whose use and application was ultimately at the discretion of the individual.* Whatever the outcome, it should *never* be seen as an invitation for the government to assume that the functional efficiency of the system was enhanced by its practices in excess. Any person who draws a paycheck in exchange for his economic contribution to the system understands these principles quite easily; they've only to look at the various payroll withholdings which determine, ultimately, his or her "take-home" pay.

"COMPLICIT IN FAILURE IS AN UNSAVORY ALLIANCE OF WILLING IGNORANCE AND ITS ARBITER - HUBRIS AND INDIFFERENCE!"

What then is the role of government, if any, in the economy? A very good question and one that was addressed in *Volume I: We Hold These Truths*. For the time being, let us simply accept the historically relevant convention that the government's role/function is specifically "enumerated" *in* the Constitution. Unfortunately, the government has (and I might add, aided by various Supreme Court decisions) selectively interpreted various provisions of the Constitution, most notably the *Commerce Clause*,[9] the *Necessary and Proper Clause*[10] and the *10th Amendment*.[11] In each case, the results of which were to the beneficial interests of selective *isms* and not unto the refining and perfecting of its construct!

---

9   Article 1, Section 8, Clause 3.

10   Article 1, Section 8, Clause 18.

11   States, simply and succinctly: "The powers not delegated to the United States by the Constitution, nor prohibited by it to the States, are reserved to the States respectively, or to the people."

"THERE ARE FEW, IF ANY, EXAMPLES WHERE LEGISLATIVE
OR JUDICIAL ACTIONS FURTHER THE CAUSE OF PERFECTING
INDIVIDUAL FREEDOM; HOWEVER THERE ARE COUNTLESS EXAMPLES
WHERE THESE ACTIONS FURTHER THE CAUSE AND INTERESTS OF
THOSE WHO FEAR THE BENEVOLENT FORCES OF FREEDOM!"

The Constitution often refers to its self-contained construct by using terms such as "enumerated herein" or "not delegated to" when speaking of rights, duties or obligations of the government or the limitation imposed thereto. It *never* exposes, even remotely, a suggestion that the government may create rights unto itself. Though the government, with the aid of the Supreme Court, may assert the claim of this privilege as being implied, the prurient assertion of its existence is insufficient grounds to assert that it does. *Due to the nature and construct of the Constitution, it is imperative to understand yet another critical point: The absence of a restriction or strictly enumerated power does not imply or otherwise suggest that a government mandate exists.* In point of fact, the complete opposite is the case: *only* those "enumerated powers" specify and relegate to the government those which *are* its *mandate!* Those not specified, as prescribed by the *10th Amendment,* are "...reserved to the States respectively, or to the People" themselves.

Let us refine the issue to a point of clarity: The Constitution does not specify nor does it grant rights to *The People,* it only specifies or "enumerates" the specific powers of the government. In other words, the document defines the government's operational limits and expressly imposes no such limitations upon the "inalienable" rights (or will) of *The People.* Yet this fundamental principle has long been ignored resulting in an aberrant form of governance.

An extension of this thought, in the most absurd manner possible, would produce the following example: I want a Ferrari yet I have not the means to possess or acquire one. However, my neighbor owns a garage which accommodates the storage of his two vehicles. A Senator discovers several Ferrari dealerships in his/her state whose success would prove, selectively, beneficial. The Senator authors legislation mandating Ferraris be awarded to persons of no means. This *bill* includes a provision requiring any person in possession of a two-car garage to surrender a space to all new Ferrari owners. This noble gesture's foundational purpose is none other than to redress the World Trade Organization's concerns as to the potential risk of the Italian government's being offended were it to find its nation's pride relegated to the elements.

This magnificent piece of insightful and conscientious legislation, funded by an excise tax on domestically produced beer, candy bars and dog chews, also includes a monthly stipend for fuel costs accompanied by several important "earmarks" and/or "appropriations" to insure the required votes of several well-meaning legislators. Now then, with deference to the intent of the Constitution, this is the very type of legislation that should be challenged however with consideration to the Supreme Courts historical tendencies, one should expect the Courts affirmation based on the now common and expansive interpretation of both the *Commerce Clause* and the *Necessary and Proper Clause.*

Consider that although this example may seem a comedic ruse, this characterization is unfortunately far more the norm than one might care to consider. The government refers to these legislative actions as *social, trade* or *stimulus* programs.

In any event, this example illustrates both the asserting (by government) of a completely fabricated *right to impose* as well as an indicator of precisely how government upsets the economic system by imposing an undue burden, among other affects, upon the system. There are many examples of these *affects* and their implications (effects). Here are the two most conspicuous:

- Extracting wealth from the economic system via *tax*.

- The redistribution, or perhaps better said, the redirection of *wealth* which then never returns to an economic cycle. This event serves to void the prospects of further economic expansion and the *regenerative force* required for productive *wealth creating* cycles.

Perhaps a more effective way to illustrate this is by yet another example identified as *the sun flower seed* metaphor: If one consumes the seed in lieu of planting it, one forgoes the multiplying benefit of the soon-to-be mature sunflower, which, when left to its *intuitive regenerative cycle* yields hundreds of sunflowers and an abundance of edible seeds.

In summation and by way of referring back to the System Operational Parameters, we can see how the violation of *Rule #2,* "The system creates no wealth beyond the value it generates." triggers economic imbalance of the system. Now, the temptation might be for one to suggest that these *social programs* are, at worst, a zero-sum gain. In other words, implying that there is neither an economic gain nor loss, i.e., referring to our Ferrari example[12], or that there is no difference as the auto dealer would have received the same benefit from a sale regardless of

---

12   This is a particularly poignant illustration especially with consideration to the "Cash for Clunkers" program created by the Federal Government in 2009 and also shows why/how it was a predictable failure.

the source of funds - be it a private party or the government. However, this would be a fallacious argument for the following reason(s): This premise ignores the significant differences between how the source of funds were created not to mention that had the *give away* not occurred, the vehicles would likely never have been sold in the first place. In the case of the private party, assuming he passes the *lawful means test,* the source of funds is from the accumulation of wealth (a component of the *wealth creation* process), whereas the government's sourcing occurs simply by the act of *taking* and then simply re-assigning or redistributing these *funds.* Also, the act of *assigning* is consistent with both *bullet* points referenced above. Again, the *sunflower seed* metaphor illustrates the relevant issues quite well supported also by Mr. Franklin's comment as presented earlier (see footnote #8).

PRACTICAL REALITIES

So then, considering the progress we've made thus far, I believe a few *practical realities* exist that are worthy of consideration.

For example: Do we let the economic system operate unchecked by the restraint of government? If so, one might ask what then are the parameters we impose on the unbridled excesses that are the tendentious nature of a *laissez-faire* economic system? How then do we subsidize the processes of government? To be sure, all very good questions and I will address each of them in due course, but first, let us review the concept of *laissez-faire* as it is most relevant to all of these questions.

The term "*laissez-faire*" is an identifying form, a phrase if you will, that has long existed in the sociology of man as a generality or as a presumed ethos. This ethos, or belief, might best be expressed in the following way: *Leave me alone to pursue my lawful and just rewards. Or, It's not broke so leave it alone and if it were, it can fix itself and if not, I will.* This strikes a chord on the instrument of self-reliance, does it not! The French, in the 1600's, crafted a colloquial expression for these notions expressed in the phrase we now know as *laissez-faire.*[13] Since that time, the term has frequently reappeared as a means to characterize that which is articulated as the consequential effect of economic excess or by what we might also refer to as *feral capitalism.*

In its contemporary uses I'm of the opinion that the term is largely misunderstood and/or misused. More acutely, *laissez-faire* in no way defines or does it represent a *trend* of economics or its excesses, if any. As a point of order, I think it more appropriate to apply the term as a practical reference to what the government *should do* versus what it *should not do.* In other words, what the government *should do is DO nothing!* Yes, there have been excesses in the economic engine of this country as well as others. They have appeared in the abusive labor practices of industry which were then met with even greater abuses; the excesses of government intervention via legislation. There has been (and there will always be) what one might view as economic excess when interpreting normal economic business cycles however, it is important to note that *extremes* such as "depressions" are not a response to "normal economic business cycles." More to the point, they are in fact most certainly and directly related to the *deliberate functions and intentions of interests who use the pliable political system to orchestrate or effectuate an advantageous or beneficial outcome.* One has only to look at U.S. monetary/banking practices to capture the truth of this statement.

---

13   The literal translation is "let do," or "leave to do," depending on which French-speaking person one asks!

Conversely, in a truly "normal"[14] business cycle the adaptable and *native kinetic forces* of an *organic* or "native economic system"[15] will trend toward minimization (if not out-right mitigation) of the impact these alleged *cycles* might otherwise have. The *native economy* accomplishes this, primarily, by or through its *intuitive response mechanisms*. I think of the *intuitive response mechanisms* in a form I identify as "tortional economic tension."[16]

The concept of *laissez-faire* is best understood in a practical application where the relevant issue is one of *organic* form and function – that is to say, leaving the economic system alone to engage in the *wealth creation* function restricted *only* by market forces. What are these market forces? Simply stated, they are the inveterate nature of the system to respond and/or to adapt to demand or changes in demand and the forces that dictate both. *Demand, not command,* is the means by which the system articulates or adjust itself to a productive result. It is simply not possible for government to affect an organic maret-response by command. The following illustrates a few of the many possible organic or native response tendancies:

1. Demand falls for an inferior product which is replaced by an im-proved version.

---

14   "Normal" business cycle: I use this term, in this instance, to identify an environment where the economic function(s) occur absent the impositions of government.

15   "Native economic system" (*native economy*): The fundamental human components that when engaged require the identifier we refer to as *economy*. These human components are inseparable from and integral to a functional organic economic system and are best described as: intuitive, self-driven and a perfecting *life sustaining source* that compel demand in search of supply.

16   "Tortional economic tension": A term that describes the organic/*native* forces applied to or con-fronted by an economic function serving to expose and eliminate deficiencies as a means to compel the refinement toward positive measured outcome. This is, in effect, the self-perfecting component of the *native economy*.

2. Buggy whip and coach manufactures retool to manufacture automobiles (a form of what is often referred to as "destructive capitalism").

3. Technological innovation spurs evolutionary applications. Example: Transistors replace digital circuitry whose application reinvigorates existing practical and related uses.

4. Toxic discharge is identified as a byproduct of a certain industry; the matter is resolved by punitive resolution through the existing judicial process. The *demand chain* applies punitive responses by/through "market response forces"[17] and the incentive for industry to adapt is effectively established. Notice: The response was not to require that legislation be passed to create the EPA or a government (i.e., taxpayer funded) "super fund" to pay for it. And,

5. It is determined that there are unfair labor practices or dangerous working environments; the matter is resolved as in "3" above. Notice again: I did not say pass legislation creating leviathans such as *OSHA, ADA* or *NLRA,*[18] – just to name a few.

Holding to, if we were sufficiently inspired, these prescriptions we must resolve then to consider that what would have evolved was indeed not an economic system as suggested by the misused phrase *laissez-faire* but, in point of fact, a purer form of capitalism. Should an enterprise or nation prefer the proven results of this type of responsive *wealth creating mechanism,* there is no substituting or manipulating of its principles (see *Rule #4.*) By the way, I'm not suggesting, as in the case of "5" above, that the intent of these legislations/regulations are without

---

17 "Market response forces" is a self-coined term used to identify the *intuitive* occurrence of an appropriately administered response by a "native economy" which tends to not tolerate abuses.

18 "OSHA:" Occupational Safety and Health Administration. "ADA:" American with Disabilities Act." "NLRA:" National Labor Relations Act 1935" – the source of "collective bargaining" rights.

merit however, consider the simple effectiveness of a judicial order/ action perfected only with the slamming of a gavel. Seems to void the need for a 3,000-page regulation and the accompanying beast-like bureaucracy!

Moreover, what I am suggesting is that not only are they (regulations) unnecessary and ever-expanding, but even more so, they create a burden to the system far beyond what possible benefit they may offer. What is certain, they've each created a perpetual and systemic form of wealth consumption. Or, more precisely stated: Although these laws are passed only once, the economic system is, by fiat, assigned a perpetual burden as each of these continuously commands a form of systemic economic *wealth consumption*. Further, the costs of administrating the agencies promulgated by these actions are not only perpetual, but the nature of government is to expand their role which in turn further expands both their scope of authority and their respective budgets. And, I might add that from all appearances, government is seemingly incapable of grasping the significance of the systemic consequence, accordingly, it executes no constructive practice to prevent or restrain its pandemic imposition.

Before moving on, I suspect there may be a lingering suspicion as to the authenticity of notions such as *wealth creation, wealth consumption, native economy* and *torsional economic tension*. I suspect further, that these terms may appear inchoate or somehow sophomoric. However, such is not the case! One has only to view each of these in the practical nature or circumstances in which, to be sure, they *organically* occur. Any individual who manages a household or business budget deals with each of these in the practice of her or his daily functions. They occur, in their most elementary form, in this way:

- *One has a demand for food to sustain his corporeal form. In order to meet this demand with a supply, one requires a means to generate funding (wealth creation) to pay for this supply (wealth consumption).*

- *If one finds himself with insufficient wealth to pay for said supply, there are effectively two choices: increase wealth or decrease or alter demand (a form of torsional economic tension).*

- *Now, if one finds that the food supply is in some way deficient, there are more choices to make; either compel the source to correct the deficiency (market response force) or select a more functional source (a self-correcting component of torsional economic tension).*

These are the basic realities occurring, with common regularity, in the *native economy*.

There is nothing ethereal or sophomoric about it, now is there? Again, we all deal with these systemic realities on a daily basis. I certainly do! No, in truth, the only ethereal or sophomoric notion is that government seems to believe your *realities* do not apply to its orchestrated version of a *contrived reality* and I believe they do!

THE CONFIRMATION OF EXCESS

As a final component of my commentary regarding *economic excesses*, I've crafted my own phrase to assist in communicating one last and critical point: *legislative coercion*. I alluded to this idea earlier when presenting the distinctions of economic cycles, *excesses* and *extremes*, one of the extremes being *depression* and the relationship to government intervention. *Legislative coercion* is the identifier for the cause that lies behind or gives rise to these types of extreme business cycles though my true intent is for it to mean something far more insidious and equally culpable. I address this, specifically, to the circumstances where a vested interest uses government to legislate beneficial reward(s) for an industry either by enabling a deliberate benefit or legislating a detrimental burden upon an opposing interest or industry. The practice of *legislative coercion,* as we have seen, has dire consequences, the nature of which we reviewed more completely in *Volume I: We Hold These Truths* in the section titled *The Policy of Conflict and Selective Ideals.*

Yet, an even greater risk than that of mischaracterizing economic forces is misdiagnosing its root cause. Far too frequently an economic motive (*capitalism*) is labeled the cause of detrimental economic effect, when in truth, few assumptions are more baseless. To assail the economic cycle as malignant is to prove the opening statement of this commentary. Further, to believe that government is capable of guarding against these abuses is to ignore its culpability!

"YES, IT IS TRUE THAT SELECT BUSINESS INTERESTS USE THE COERCIVE LEGISLATIVE FEATURE OF GOVERNMENT TO PROMOTE THEIR ECONOMIC INTERESTS. HOWEVER, WHAT IS FAR LESS CONSPICUOUS AND FAR MORE DAMAGING IS THAT THESE VERY INTERESTS USE GOVERNMENT TO SHIELD THEM FROM THEIR GREATEST FEAR OF ALL: FREE MARKET FORCES!"

In much the same way as business;

"INTRUSIVE AND COERCIVE GOVERNMENT'S GREATEST FEAR
IS THE MARKET FORCES OF FREEDOM AND THUS IT ORIENTS
ITS CONSIDERABLE FORCE TO INSURE THE OPPOSITION
POSSESSES AS LITTLE INFLUENCE AS POSSIBLE!"

Holding to the belief that this statement may be formative in scope, I suspect that upon thorough review there may be very few legislative or government entrails emerging from this functional filter. Moreover, canvassing the contours of our own social landscape, consider the most alarming scourge of all: *the multitudes of our fellow Americans who actually believe that the dysfunction of our system is a systemic byproduct of its nature, when in reality it is a supremely effective barometer of its abuse!*

However, for purposes of affirming the present context, I will provide, in the comment that follows, an example of this abhorrent form:

It is often said that the depression of the 1930's was brought about by the stock market crash of 1929 though I must confess I'm of the opinion that nothing could be further from the truth. The stock market crash was only the visible consequence of a far greater cause. The *cause,* I suggest, being the consequence of crafted events providing the vehicle for a massive explosion/accumulation of debt accommodated by predatory monetary policies, enabled by the federal government and orchestrated by the Federal Reserve Bank. In reality, the federal government enabled these policies by way of legislation that was promulgated by influential forces further up the command structure. This should sound strangely familiar!

The legislation I speak of is none other than the Federal Reserve Act of 1913. The supreme benefactor and driving force behind the Act was, primarily, John Pierpont Morgan, Jr. though not to the exclusion of other American and European financiers. These gentlemen *used* the system to assist in the financing of Great Britain's, among others, involvement in World War I for which they were well rewarded. However, as Great Britain[19] began to suffer the effects of their own manipulative monetary policies, among these being the attempt to revalue their currency, a rippling economic effect migrated throughout Europe and the U.S. banking system. The Federal Reserve and participating institutions, attempting to both protect and advance their interests, began flooding the British financial markets with cash. Knowing, as financiers do, that there is profit and control to be accumulated in crisis, why not simply create or take advantage of one? Consider of course that when one controls monetary policy, crisis is just one of the many tools at your disposal and the flashpoint for this event was ignited by key Federal Reserve affiliate banks which was to simply "call" (or *accelerate*) for the payoff of various loans. Consequently many individuals and firms found themselves in a non-liquid (with few or no cash reserves) position. Having few, if any, options available to meet the demands of these banks, debtors were abruptly forced to sell off assets (bonds, securities, etc.) and the sudden flood of "sell" orders triggered the collapse of the "market." Short version: The Bank of England fiasco triggered the global monetary collapse, in part, creating the rich opportunity environment for crafting of a *crisis* which was the *calling due* of various loans. The sell off of assets, to meet the demands of the bankers, triggered the stock market collapse of October of 1929[20].

---

19   It is important to know that the British Central Bank operates in much the same was as the Federal Reserve does in the U.S. – both are private banking concerns.

20   This statement, though accurate as a summation, does not address all of the contributing factors. As well, there was far more collateral damage to the U.S. financial/economic/political system than simply the stock market "crash."

The correlative and aggregate value of the events leading up to the *Crash of 1929*, along with those since and through the first quarter of 2009, should impress one with an overwhelming sense of disgust (unless of course you are an international financier). I am specifically referring to the practices of *legislative coercion* the contemporary version of which - and there are others such as the *Financial Modernization Act of 1999* which are equally culpable - are the series of "bailouts" provided the financial system (beginning in the second quarter of 2008) that preceded the stock market collapse (beginning in the fourth quarter of the same year). As Yogi Berra said, "This is like déjà vu all over again!"

Over the years I've read and studied many books and countless commentaries on the Great Depression, the fore and aftermath, and the dominant message of nearly all identifies the culprit as political malfeasance and errant monetary policy. This comment will or should neither stun nor surprise the student of political and economic policy/ history. For what reason? Economies and their mediums of exchange are always predictable. The unfortunate reality of this observation is also expressed in this way:

> "The greatest consequence occurs from having ignored the signals that indicate that there will be a predictable consequence!"

And so I trust that being armed, as you now are, with the aid of the preceding commentaries, when one hears our economic system characterized as abusive, dysfunctional and predatory, you will know with absolute certainty that capitalism, not unlike the republican form of government, is not the culprit! Similarly, as in the practices of our government (which is republican in name only), our economic system has equally been the victim of malignant divisiveness and misdirection. It is, to be precise, the *function* and not the *form* that is the predator!

Once again I draw on the clarity of history to authenticate this point to a necessary degree of precision. Perhaps, arguably, no one single individual in American history understood the practical and aggregate fallout of *errant monetary policy* better than President Andrew Jackson.

> "*It is to be regretted that the rich and powerful too often bend the acts of government to their selfish purposes.* Distinctions in society will always exist under every just government. Equality of talents, of education, or of wealth can not be produced by human institutions. In the full enjoyment of the gifts of Heaven and the fruits of superior industry, economy, and virtue, every man is equally entitled to protection by law; but when the laws undertake to add to these natural and just advantages artificial distinctions, to grant titles, gratuities, and exclusive privileges, to make the rich richer and the potent more powerful, the humble members of society — the farmers, mechanics, and laborers — who have neither the time nor the means of securing like favors to themselves, have a right to complain of the injustice of their government. *There are no necessary evils in government. Its evils exist only in its abuses.* If it would confine itself to equal protection, and, as Heaven does its rains, shower its favors alike on the high and the low, the rich and the poor, it would be an unqualified blessing.*"

President Jackson's comments project a clarifying aspect to the conversation and provide a suitable endorsement for my suggestion that the term *legislative coercion* is quite appropriate. It is from the desire to void the tendency of coercive government that we should prefer government to *let do* so that the economic engine might function to its perfection and not *let* government *do just anything*. From my studies of political economic history I have resolved to the following observation, which has become a rule unto itself:

"INDIVIDUAL INTERESTS AND ECONOMIC MOTIVES MERGE IN THE ARMATURE OF POLITICAL INFLUENCE- THE OUTCOME OF WHICH APPEARS AND IS ALWAYS CHARACTERIZED AS MERE COINCIDENCE!"

It is for this reason, among others, I believe that with consideration to our present economic and political climate we are at an extreme risk for yet another *manufactured crisis* and one that will most assuredly redefine both American history and its future. It will appear both as if a coincidence and as the ultimate and supreme savior whose adoption will be offered as the only possible solution. It will appear as both an economic and political solution the consequence of which will be the complete and total surrender of what remains of your sovereign rights. You will be called upon to express the convictions of your conscience in order to repel this nefarious attempt, I pray that you will![21] When that time comes I trust you will recall the following excerpt from *Volume: I:*

"HOW CAN WE PROFESS THAT WE ARE TRULY A FREE AND JUST PEOPLE WHEN FREEDOM AND JUSTICE ARE NO LONGER OUR PRACTICE OR AMONG THE CHOICES OFFERED?"

We have now arrived at this critical point, but first, let us restate a fundamental principle:

---

21   This issue will be discussed more fully in a latter chapter entitled: "The Outcome and Psychology of Monetary Conquest."

"THE EXTENT TO WHICH AN ECONOMY IS FUNCTIONALLY
VIBRANT IS THE EXTENT TO WHICH WEALTH CREATION EXCEEDS
WEALTH CONSUMPTION. IT TRULY IS THAT SIMPLE!"

It is from this fundamental axiom, in part, that we derive the means by which we pay for government and it is the reason why government, not the *economic system,* should be restrained! All too often aberrations occurring out of errant judgment are met with idiotic notions such as *regulation* or *deregulation* either, or both, often being classified as either too much or not enough. In truth, either approach is formed from or out of economic bias and completely absent of intellectual balance or rational thought. The aroma of indignant rancor is never a stranger when the time comes for political accountability. The finger pointing wages fierce derisiveness and the side with fewest fingers always looses! *Strange, and I should think you might agree, is the case that so many people find themselves represented by so few fingers!*

"IN THE END, WHAT IS LOST IS MADE MOST CLEAR BY
ITS ABSENCE AND WHAT IS ABSENT IS CHARACTER!"

GOVERNMENT FUNDING MECHANISMS

The question of how best to pay for government is answered in a manner not all that different from how any enterprise (or individual) answers the very same inquiry. It will likely come as no surprise, once again, that the Constitution provided the framework for the government to be a self-sustaining enterprise. The intent was that government would generate revenues as an attendant to the economic system which is accomplished through various tariffs on trade and/or excise taxes generated from commerce. As in the case of the model I've previously discussed, one might suggest that as an integral component of the *wealth creation process,*

It is by no means a coincidence that the individual income tax system's appearance closely parallels the ascension of increased practices and frequency of legislative coercion, along with the accelerated shifting of tax burden away from corporate interests. Again, there is not such thing as coincidence in politics!

It is also within the mandate of government to generate revenues for services rendered on a *fee for service* basis. However, as with any dying economy, it is most often the case that the demands placed upon the system, in this instance by the government, have expanded far beyond its *operational parameters* and the productive output of the economic system (refer to the *System Operational Parameters* in the previous section).Various interests surface with persuasive arguments that government should do *this* and the government should do *that* with absolutely no consideration as to *constitutional limits* or the funds required to pay for these breaches of conscience.

However, not wanting to stand on or obstruct the process by suggesting seemingly inconsequential points of order and/or not wanting to appear insensitive to the demands of these interests, the legislators happily provide access to the ever-reaching and ever-lengthening arm of government all under the auspices of *for the good of the people.* Yes, always for the good of the people, but never, strangely, is the newly created and expanded role ever perfected with the *consent* of the people who pay for it!

There are other common expressions that are the product of the *ism* factory which have made their way in to the lexicon of political rhetoric as well. But there are few more deceptive than the commonly used phrase, "The People have the right to…." The right to a home, the right to free health care, the right to free medicine, the right to retirement benefits and the list goes on and on. Well, as my darling mother used to say, "If you can pick it off the money tree, you can have it!" Why is it mothers understand economics yet their children who become politicians do not?

Needless to say, along with the newly discovered role of government comes the need to find new sources of revenues to pay for it! Inevitably, the problem becomes one where not only are existing government resources unable to meet the growing financial demands of the benevolent legislature, there were and are always industries who feel that existing revenue generating practices are detrimental to their interests. This of course leaves only one reasonable choice; to summarily dispense with many of these practices (mostly tariffs) and favorably alter corporate tax rates using many a false and abhorrent premise each ably provided by influential and conscientious sources.[22] From this result was born both the newly created right of government to tax income (individual) and the American form of class warfare and its toxic legacy continues to this day. Of course, the government demands not met by tax revenues are easily provided for by the Federal Reserve Bank. We will discuss this issue further in a later section titled *Monetary Policy.*

In keeping with the economic model previously presented, it is important to consider that the tax system is one of the single greatest

---

22   There are wonderful examples of these crafty presentations in the Congressional Record. The reading is very enlightening particularly those relating to Agricultural Subsidies and Financial Services Industry.

forms of *wealth consumption* in the U.S. exceeded only by government *deficit spending* and *debt accumulation* practices. Yet even the tax system has not escaped the consequences of *legislative coercion,* the influences of which have rendered the tax code supremely biased, largely indiscernible, irretrievably deficient and systemically dysfunctional. Setting aside the constitutional issues relating to its legitimacy and resting on the practical points alone, the approach to funding government by way of a tax on Individual income is, as it has proven to be, far too easily manipulated, a tactical and economic disincentive and functionally unmanageable. The management and administrative costs of the tax system alone are also a form of *wealth consumption* which I find strangely unnerving as one considers that its function is blithely defined as *revenue generating.* It is a testament to the dysfunction of our federal and state governments that this revenue generating system exists at all.

Yes, it is important that government should never be permitted to function beyond its mandate. However, it is even more important that government should never be able to change, expand or create its own mandate(s). As we have seen by the effect(s) of far too many wayward interests:

"WHEN GOVERNMENT IS ABLE TO ASSUME A RIGHT TO
GOVERN SIMPLY BY THE CLAIM THAT IT CAN, IT WILL NOT
BE LONG BEFORE IT WILL ALSO LICENSE IMPULSE RESPONSE
IS RARELY CONSIDERATE, MEASURED OR FUNCTIONAL."

Yet when using the impulse bias of economic class warfare even the most reasoned individual will find alliance with government appearing as, *Give unto myself that which I can take from another* form of governance. There are nearly countless government programs that mirror this practice and this ruse is completely destructive both in form and function.

By way of teasing a discussion relating to entitlement programs in a later section of this volume, what follows are a few conspicuous examples not only of the *form* where government *assumes a right to govern* but also the monetary and economic abuses that result:

- *Medicare (entire program).* In 1967, the House Ways and Means Committee predicted that the new Medicare program, launched the previous year, would cost about $12 billion in 1990. Actual Medicare spending in 1990 was $110 billion—off by nearly a factor of 10.[23]

- *ESRD program.* In 1972, Congress enacted a universal entitlement to kidney dialysis for patients suffering from end stage renal disease. The program proved twice as expensive as the publicly predicted levels—$229 million in 1974 instead of the predicted $100 million. The bill's authors had seriously underestimated the demand for services, especially among the over-65 population.[24]

- *Medicaid DSH program.* In 1987, Congress estimated that Medicaid's disproportionate share hospital (DSH) payments—which states use to provide relief to hospitals that serve especially large numbers of Medicaid and uninsured patients—would cost less than $1 billion in 1992. The actual cost that year was a staggering $17 billion. Among other

23   Joint Economic Committee: Senator Sam Brownback, Ranking Republican Member, July 31, 2009 – Report: "Are Health Care Reform Cost Estimates Reliable?"

24   ibid

things, federal lawmakers had failed to detect loopholes in the legislation that enabled states to draw significantly more money from the federal treasury than they would otherwise have been entitled to claim under the program's traditional 50-50 funding scheme.[25]

- *Medicare homecare benefit.* When Congress debated changes to Medicare's homecare benefit in 1988, the projected 1993 cost of the benefit was $4 billion. The actual 1993 cost was more than twice that amount, $10 billion.[26]

- *Medicare catastrophic coverage benefit.* In 1988, Congress added a catastrophic coverage benefit to Medicare, to take effect in 1990. In July 1989, the Congressional Budget Office (CBO) doubled its cost estimate for the program, for the four-year period 1990-1993, from $5.7 billion to $11.8 billion. CBO explained that it had received newer data showing it had significantly under-estimated prescription drug cost growth, and it warned Congress that even this revised estimate might be too low. This was a principal reason Congress repealed the program before it could take effect.[27]

- *SCHIP.* In 1997, Congress established the State Children's Health Insurance Program as a capped grant program to states, and appropriated $40 billion to be doled out to states over 10 years at a rate of roughly $5 billion per year, once implemented. In each year, some states exceeded their allotments, requiring shifts of funds from other states that

---

25   ibid
26   ibid
27   ibid

had not done so. By 2006, unspent reserves from prior years were nearly exhausted. To avert mass dis-enrollments, Congress decided to appropriate an additional $283 million in FY 2006 and an additional $650 million in FY 2007.[28]

- *Massachusetts Commonwealth Care.* In 2006, the Bay State passed a historic *universal-coverage* plan, which combined a mandate on all residents to have health coverage with generous subsidies for lower-income uninsured families. At that time, the program was predicted to cost roughly $472 million in fiscal year 2008. It cost $628 million that year.[29]

Needless to say, these are only programs that generally deal with the government's systemic fallacy of what constitutes social engineering. Moreover, it is but one small yet obscenely expensive component of a pathological expression serving best to indicate how and in what way government can be both the soldier and the originator of *coercive forces* that completely disfigure a functional economic system. Considering these examples (above) as comparative fodder for the filtering function of the Systemic Operational Parameters, what follows are but (only) a few examples of how/why this occurs.

- Social programs are, in effect, nothing more than a form of income redistribution. These concepts imply a form of economic reapportionment that creates the illusion of benefit. However, as we can see from the examples above, not only are they artificial benefits, their actual costs are far greater than the measureable economic benefit actually delivered. This is caused by the *add on* costs, which I refer to

---

28 ibid
29 ibid

as the "Systemic Cost Multiplier Effect",[30] a component of "Physio-Sociological Economics" (PSE)[31] effect.

- All government programs result in the removal of any tangible forces that traditionally accompany an economic cycle. As government programs excise these *forces* from the economic cycle, participants no longer impose upon themselves the prudent affects of monetary burden. Consequently, when given the option of self-control vs. no economic or monetary consequence (i.e., the service is now free), they will tend toward choosing the latter, no cost-*no burden, option.*

- All government programs place an exponential cost burden upon the *native economy.* A perfect examples of this is privately funded health care costs; as the government has migrated into the health care provider domain, its approach to *cost control* (ignoring for the moment the component of government sponsored health care related to explosive costs caused by waste and graft) has been to lower reimbursement costs for services. The effect of this has forced the health care system to recoup the non-recovered costs of the government sponsored component by shifting these costs to the so called "*private,* i.e., non-government, health care consumer. And lastly, for now;

---

30 Systemic Cost Multiplier Effect: This concept attempts to comprise the unforeseen yet predictable economic costs associated with government programs. It is an organic feature of *PSE* and identifies the quantitative effects accompanying the absence of "tortional economic forces" inherent in government sponsored programs.

31 Physio-Sociological Economics (PSE): I use this term to identify the practices and tendencies of how economic actions/events or enterprises orient themselves, intuitively, addressing or responding to sociological/political preferences or issues. The motive force is typically one of an advantage-driven response (type) form.

- The most severe and lasting consequence of government programs is the *Physio-Sociological-Economic (PSE)* effect. This is the component of government spending that is largely ignored; it is also the component that is the most costly and whose effects are pervasive and lasting. It is both, in its simplest form, the nature of industry (business) to participate in an economic cycle that produces wealth and the manner in which it configures/adapts its industry in response to opportunity. As government, most conspicuous in the post-WWI era, has no economic consequence, duty or perceived monetary/financial limitations, it also has no impulse-control on spending. The consequence of this is the complete absence of what I have previously referred to as *tortional economic forces* which would otherwise tend to restrain and/or perfect its spending practices. Thus, industry adapts to the free-flow of funds which has its own consequence as well. In short, now able to control and rely on government funding, business itself no longer needs to address the *tortional economic forces* which would traditionally and otherwise refine the efficiency of their *economic cycle.* The result of this is that business then adapts to the *feeding frenzy* caused by the free-flow of government funds which produces both explosive program costs and severely degrades the quality of services. This is by no means an exhaustive study of such consequences. However, there is one final effect I believe to be worth pointing out: The detrimental constriction in and upon the *native economic wealth creation* enterprise component. In the most basic form, the effect appears in this way: As enterprise has adapted to the course of least resistance (i.e., government sponsored programs), where it no longer has the burden of efficiency/ productivity, these enterprises resign from the practice of developing or enhancing their services or product line for the non-government market. Moreover, *the consumption of wealth* effects, caused by excessive government spending, further restricts the flow of capital that would otherwise seek returns by/from investing in research and development that is an integral and necessary part of the *wealth creation* cycle of an adaptive and vibrant economy.

"THE SUSPENSION OF ABUSE REQUIRES THE
SURRENDER OF ENTITLEMENTS LICENSE!"

Using the basic components of the previous observations as a filter, one requires only a token application of effort to observe the risks and consequences of governmental economic intrusions. However, whether it is military, education or any of the thousands of government entitlement/social programs, the cost is not only measured in dollars, it is also measured in the loss of economic freedom and the qualitative form of good and sound governance.

Government, like any enterprise that wants to be functional, must operate within its means. Returning the function of government to the limits of it structure and its means then restores the function of government to be, once again, servant of the people. Tying the means (revenue sources) of government to the wealth creating engine then relegates the government to its appropriate domain. We might even suggest that this appropriate domain be that of an advocate of freedom and prosperity *not* its executioner. The federal and state governments must resume the role of affirming and insuring that economic interests accrue to this country's benefit and not to that of another's.

> "INEQUALITY IN THE PRACTICE OF TRADE IS NOT MADE
> EQUITABLE BY IGNORING INEQUALITY REGARDLESS
> OF WHAT YOUR TRADING PARTNER MIGHT SAY!"

Again, government revenues need to be tied to the productivity of the national *economic wealth creating system;* doing so assists in the desire to restore the republican form of government as defined by the U.S. Constitution. As can be seen from the view of historical clarity and by observing its contemporary practices, our government has clearly demonstrated that it is *incapable of functional and rational allegiance* to its construct. Unfortunately, the devolution of our government's functional practices is directly related to its own unique brand of monetary policy.

> "THE IDEA OF FREE MONEY, THE ILLUSION THAT SPENDING IS
> THE SAME AS WEALTH AND THAT DEBT ACCUMULATIONS ARE
> EQUIVALENT TO AND ALSO A MEASURE OF ECONOMIC GROWTH
> NOT ONLY PRODUCE INSOLVENCY IN PRACTICE, THEY ARE EQUALLY
> INSOLVENT AT THEIR THEORETICAL CORE! TO BE EVEN MORE
> PRECISE, THE GREATEST ILLUSION OF ALL IS THE PERCEPTION
> THAT THE ABILITY TO BORROW IS THE EQUIVALENT OF WEALTH!"

The arbiter of these fiscal and monetary policies espouses these as both revolutionary and evolutionary doctrines with the effervescence of a mystic, yet when the mist fades and reason prevails the dangers and the limitations become abundantly transparent. I've spent most of my professional career working in professions directly or indirectly affected by government extremes and practices masquerading as monetary policy. I know of these "extremes" and I've seen first hand their "practices" in action by observing how billions upon billions of dollars have been made by and through the process. I've known the faces of the victors and the scared vanquished and there is no, absolutely no valor in this type of economic or political conquest!

> "THERE IS NO VALUE CREATED WHEN THERE IS NO
> VALUE EXCHANGED. THIS BRAND OF COMMERCE
> IS BUT AN ILLUSION, A SLIGHT OF HAND!"

In short, this is not hyperbole, suspicion or rank curiosity, this is a function of not only academics but more importantly, real-world knowledge and it comes from a perspective not of *I think* but from the strength and certainty of *I know!* The federal government, and by adoption of the same practices many of the states, has engaged in this perpetual binge fueled by the notion of debt-funded spending. The government and many special interest groups will claim or assert that you should have a certain benefit as a *right* and the people are lured further into the something-for-nothing scheme amounting to nothing more than predatory leverage, or in simpler terms, *the taking* from one *to give* to another – all of which seems quite satisfactory. After all, you're entitled – you've earned it! I'm not sure how and in what way it was earned though it is my hope that perhaps someone, someday, will be able to offer a reasonably sound explanation.

The government, always delighted to keep you distracted, uninformed and satisfied, is only too happy to acquire your ignorant silence by anesthetizing you with a little handout now and then. And, of course, you're quite happy to accept it; after all, it costs you nothing (or so it would seem). I refer to this form of thinking as *practical detachment*, which I define as *the evolutionary and enlightened belief that one's duty, responsibility or preferential outcome may be assigned to another. It also carries with it the presumption that there are no consequences for any less than desirable outcome.*

I am, by way of a form of satirical reference, tendering for your consideration that perhaps this era and its practices must be put to an end! If our collective intentions trend toward prosperity, then the course we must navigate can only be that which relies on proven economic and monetary principles. There is no other choice.

I'm reminded of a story a friend of mine told me many years ago. Somehow it seems relevant, I'll let you be the judge: Seems there was an older fellow who would spend the afternoon sitting on his front porch swing. A young boy, on his way home from school, would stop and visit for a time and often as the young boy was preparing to leave, the old man's Bloodhound would raise its head and make a yelping sort of howl. As the weeks and months passed the boy's curiosity finally peaked and he asked, "Hey Mister, why's that old hound of yours yelp so much?" The old man responded by saying "Well, ya see, he's lay'n on a nail!" Struck by the old man's response the boy asks, "Well then why don't he get up and move?" The old man replied, "Don't hurt 'nough I guess!"

The point being; perhaps the reason we Americans permit these abuses is simply because, as yet, it simply "Don't hurt 'nough, I guess!"

Simple economics is really quite simple! Once the veneer of incomprehensibility and theoretical regiments are stripped, the truth of the matter is that the arcana exist only within the cloistered environs of academia and at the government level. Being economically or fiscally prudent is not the same as *doing without* an item or *doing with* that of another; no, simple economics is something quite different! It is, at the end of the day, the satisfaction that accompanies knowing that you have earned and possess the product of your efforts both of which are yours and yours to do with as you please!

I am a believer in the power of the human mind and its many gifts but mostly, I treasure our intuitive sense of self-reliance and its profound nature which I believe is best described as both our *native goodness* and *inspired genius!* This is the *image* I hold. However, we must always remember this:

> "...THE ONCE LASTING IMAGE, HAVING LOST THE
> VALIANT, SILENTLY FADES AND IMAGINES NO MORE."

In truth, the economic form we know as *capitalism* is *not* the product of *theoretical economics* formed in the labyrinth of academia. It is neither a form unto itself nor a *model* looking for a willing cog. Yes, many interpreted this form as a *system* or *model* but again, these are theoretical attempts to both qualify and quantify what occurs only in the free exchange of an idea and its physical form, *commodity.* As we see in life, and in many different instances where man believes that concomitant with his ability to describe an occurrence, what then follows is his assumption that he may also will, control and/or otherwise regulate that to which he assigns a defining characteristic. It is, arguably, that by holding to this feeble-minded premise (i.e. *control* is the supreme arbiter of *dominion)* we become the primary cause for the various forms of imbalance we observe and endure socially, politically and economically.

As we discussed in *Volume I: We Hold These Truths*, the concepts of *freedom* are not the arbitrary notions of man but conveyed only from the benevolent will of a *Presence* or *Being* we predominantly refer to as the *Creator*. Likewise, the concept we identify as *capitalism* is truly and only the extension of a free person, freely expressing his or her "inalienable rights" and doing so with a fundamental adherence to the understanding that though one may be free to express his interests, he is not at liberty to express a right or freedom beyond the point where doing so adversely affects the *inalienable rights* of another.

There is nothing mysterious or abstract about a functional economic system or, for that matter, the environment required for it to foster and propagate its beneficial rewards. What is, however, mysterious, is the seemingly unexplainable tendency of a system of government, so perfectly designed to be its advocate, yet preferring to be the instrument of its destruction.

After all, it truly is *Simple Economics!*

Let's proceed, shall we!

In preparation for what follows and with consideration to this presentation entitled *Simple Economics*, I would ask that you, the reader, record in your minds and consider the significance of the two following quotes, paying particular attention to their sources.

The first is from the economist John Kenneth Galbraith:

> *"The study of money, above all other fields in economics,*
> *is one in which complexity is used to disguise truth or to*

evade truth, not to reveal it. The process by which banks
create money is so simple that the mind is repelled."

The last is from Mayer A. Rothschild, the patriarch of the Rothschild dynasty and a 17th century financier:

"Let me issue and control a nation's money
and I care not who writes the laws."

And so, as in all things, there is a *cause* for all that occurs and an equal measure of reason for why it does!

Monetary Policy

AS IS THE CASE WITH MANY ASPECTS of our daily lives, it is the ordinary and somewhat everyday occurrences that seem to blend into the background and become accepted practice and customs accompanying our every action. They occur with such a high degree of repetitiveness that we barely take notice of their significance. They are *gray*, non-descript items, events or assumptions. Who among us pays attention to the double yellow line on the expressway or pays mind to the presumed notion that it implies? Yet we drive in opposite directions of one another at combined speeds in excess of 120 miles per hour and never question that an oncoming driver will not honor the presumed notion of the double yellow line! Do you ever think of having to tell your heart to beat or your lungs to draw a breath? Of course not, your autonomic nervous system takes care of that function for you and requires nary a conscious thought.

No, the only time we ever consider these anonymous customs and actions is when an alarm sounds, when something runs afoul! A driver, for whatever reason, crosses the double yellow line and the outcome of course begets the (likely) tragedy of a head-on collision. In the case of your lungs or heart, it occurs with a sudden schism or alarm: respiratory or heart failure. Then, in these instances, we take notice and struggle for an explanation for *the why* such things occur or *the what* for what went wrong! We only pay attention to seemingly insignificant items as a matter of necessity and when we do, we discover that they are, in point of fact, quite significant after all.

"IT IS NOT IN SILENCE WE ARE REMINDED OF WHAT
IS CRITICAL; IT IS IN THE AFTERMATH OF CRISIS WE
REDISCOVER THERE ARE NO EXCEPTIONS!"

Monetary policy appears quite benign and seemingly insignificant in the customs and action of everyday occurrences all the while blending seamlessly with the contour of the landscape and we pay little or no attention to the goings on of its function or the practices and organisms which lie behind its construct. I would suggest that in this instance, even when the alarm sounds, few would even consider this subject *(monetary policy)* worthy of reconsideration. It is so *gray* and non-descript an issue that it may be more accurate to say it is so nondescript that few will even dare approach the subject. Yes, there is much dialogue employing the phrase *monetary policy* and to be sure, as a conversation piece it generates a great deal of media traffic. Yet, the most critical issues regarding the subject continue to be elusive as if the underlying message is:

"AS LONG AS WE DON'T SAY WHAT IT IS, WE CAN
MAKE IT MEAN WHATEVER WE WANT!"

An element of fear and apprehension lurks behind the door labeled *monetary policy* and those who attempt to engage in meaningful discourse are summarily labeled quacks and purposefully fade into obscurity. The 2008 presidential campaign season offers an example. I sat in on several group discussions that followed the televised debates and were one to have elected a candidate purely on the grounds of constitutional knowledge, Congressman Ron Paul[32] shines most bril-

---

32   This is not necessarily an endorsement of the Congressmen. It is more a statement about *conspicuous by its absence.* On an issue of such importance, why is it so conspicuously avoided?

liantly, which leads me to the very point I want to make: Arguably the most structurally sound candidate, that is, one who understands – and it would appear is willing to honor – the nation's founding principles and simultaneously grasps the fundamental components of a working financial structure, is barely given notice. Even in rebuttal, I found only one candidate able to acknowledge the congressman's insights. The point being is that when a frank and direct discussion is presented on the subject, the participants run for cover and the worthy messenger, in this case Congressman Ron Paul, is relegated to obscurity. It would seem that the scale tips to the side of political survivability so as to masterfully avoid substantive dialogue.

"THE PRACTICE OF POLITICS IS TO ESCAPE THE TOUGH QUESTIONS SO AS TO AVOID HAVING TO BE ACCOUNTABLE FOR THE ANSWERS!"

I offer the previous comments deliberately as a prelude to what follows in order to establish a basis for what I hope you, the reader, will find a meaningful and manageable discussion on a subject that is typically painfully boring. Further, it is frequently one that will set an otherwise patient and inquisitive person to thoughts of doing yard-work or flossing one's teeth! I've attempted to confine the subject to the very basics and avoid languishing in tedious analytical conversation and I fully acknowledge that by doing so I will likely suffer the wrath of the highly misinformed. However, I've not endeavored to please the segment that will undoubtedly object, primarily as I fully expect that their commitment to maintaining their stature will confine them to considering only their perspective. It is the equivalent of attempting to teach pigs to sing; it frustrates the dickens out of the teacher and irritates the pig. And why, you might ask? Because pigs don't sing! In the end, I ask that you force yourself to read and understand what follows; it is the cornerstone for rehabilitating our present circumstance so that we might enjoy a much brighter future. This subject ties what you have read to this point, including *Volume I* of this series, to all that follows.

I see great opportunity in the world, and as a country or as a people who are the lone stewards who must guard the sacred fire of liberty, our work is clearly far from being complete. It might even be more appropriate to say that if we were to be graded on the effectiveness of our *watch*, our performance would likely be rewarded with an extended stay at *Leavenworth*[33]. Need I remind: *Great blessings are accompanied by an equal measure of burden.* Some, however, would have you believe that *burden* implies a *duty* to give away that which you have earned and I believe that presumption to be both ignorant and disingenuous. Ignorant as it lacks the understanding of what a *blessing* is and *disingenuous* because they would prefer to see you give away that which you have earned rather than *give* of themselves so that they, and others, might also accrue the very same reward.

> "OURS IS NOT THE BURDEN OF GIVING A HANDOUT; IT IS, HOWEVER, FOR EACH TO BE WILLING TO INSPIRE OTHERS BY THEIR ACTIONS SUCH THAT ALL THAT MAY BE REQUIRED IS THE SIMPLE GESTURE OF GIVING A HAND UP!"

No, this country's burden is not wealth or the mandate of its redistribution; it is, instead, the timeliness of democracy evolving! Evolving to and perfecting by its practice the universal recognition that "...all men are created equal and endowed by their creator...." This, my fellow Americans, is the *blessing*. Our great burden is that we are to perfect this ideal not only by our ascending to its call but even more, it is that

---

33 Leavenworth, Kansas: The location of the federal (U.S.) penitentiary.

we are to plant this seed and see to its tending such that it becomes yet another blessing (to others) and yet another. By doing so there will yet come a day where there will be no room for the tyrant and no room for the taking because in the mind of all mankind, on the door of every home, of every business and in every hall of every government and on the bench of every court there will be a placard upon which the following word will appear: *Emancipation!* This is democracy at its core. This is the only *ism* we can *Stand4*.

Democracy is neither the giving of a *thing* or the taking of a *value;* it is only the recognition and regard for what is *noble*, what is *virtuous*, what is *righteous* and defending another from the assault of their taking! It is when faced with the opportunity of conquest, even should the ambition rests on the principal of righteousness, one elects the action that resolves to what is deferential to an *inalienable right*.

With thoughtful consideration to the previous comment, I am reminded of two specific occasions in the life of George Washington. The first is in March of 1783 and well past the battle of Yorktown. The Continental Army remains *in the field* and many of the officers and troops have endured nearly two years without pay and with no sign of any resolution as to their promised pensions. An anonymous letter had been circulated calling on the officers to meet in a log hut for a vote on a planned action to overthrow the Continental Congress and install a military government. General Washington,[34] having intercepted the letter, made an unexpected appearance at a meeting of his officers. Invoking his authority by strategically recalling the glory of their col-

---

34   General George Washington, Newburgh, NY, March 15, 1783: The concept of what is *fortuitous* is often not fully understood until many years after an event, marking its occurrence, has taken place. It would seem that the significance of the general's appearance before his officers has been long forgotten and as an enduring instrument for conveying a greater sense of the concept I reference above, I have included his comments in the *Appendix*. I suggest it be read and pondered for its significance.

lective journey and the virtue of patriotism, he persuaded the officers to set aside their ambitions for the sake of posterity. The second, which defines the presidential transition (of office) to this day, was at the conclusion of his second term, quietly and unceremoniously retiring to his beloved Mt. Vernon.

Two seemingly inconspicuous *gray*[35] events illustrating the idea of *giving* so that the seeds of freedom might yet yield abundantly. This is the example of an individual's *burden* being demonstrated in the giving of his own unique *blessing*. This nation and our world is starving for this type of *selfless leadership*.

Then of course, there is Thomas Jefferson, who more than any, before or since, best understood this ideal. He understood the philosophical core of its still and dormant seed. There are many reasons to admire President Jefferson, but for me, it is for this one reason that I regard him so highly and have studied the man to the degree that I have. It is from his clarity, his understanding of the anthropological form that his words are (still) so very important:

> *"I sincerely pray that all the members of the human*
> *family may, in the time prescribed by the Father*
> *of us all, find themselves securely established in the*
> *enjoyment of life, liberty, and happiness."*

---

35   In this instance I'm identifying the use of the word *gray* in the context as it appears in the opening paragraph of this chapter.

A PRELUDE OF PERSPECTIVE

In a discussion on *monetary policy*, one might find this introduction rather peculiar. However I assure you it is quite relevant. Money is only an instrument of exchange, a tool not unlike a hammer or a sword that can be either an instrument that conveys value or one whose allure compels that it be used to take it. Through the discussion that follows, the reader will become aware of how this instrument functions and why its use and the methodology surrounding the same needs to be clearly understood and deliberately restrained. It is no understatement to suggest that the future, not only of this country but also that of other nations as well, will be determined by our crafting not only a better understanding, but more to the point, a better and more fundamentally sound *monetary practice*. In mapping a course for what is to come, I can think of few items more appropriately placed at the top of any *to-do* list particularly when considering the ideas discussed to this point.

It has been and continues to be my ultimate design that this composition not be characterized as academic but more a blending of historically significant references with economic and political philosophy most deliberately being from the view of a pragmatist. Do consider then that it is only my intention in what follows to give a brief and somewhat anecdotal composition of *money's origins, fundamental money mechanics* and the *business of banking and finance*. All with the intention of arriving at a point of clarity which is to illustrate that *monetary policy* is not at all complex when one considers it from the perspective of its *core fundamentals*. It is only from the lips of the politician and the financier that the subject assumes the appearance of complexity. In the case of the former (politician), it is more likely the case that it is not an issue of complexity but more likely a lack of interest or comprehension, or both. This might explain the reason for the spellbinding gaze when faced with the obstacles accompanying any effort to restore a measure of *monetary discipline*. From the financier's perspective, the confusion offers a uniquely beneficial effect as well. I have always enjoyed the news clips of Alan Greenspan,[36] particularly when one studies and understands how *disinformation* and *fear* are used by the system to great effect. It is, after all, a business and one that revolves strictly around the *for-profit and control* model the success of which is mastered only from the strength of the financier's (banker's) ability to control the environment in which the business operates and profits.

"CONSIDER THAT A MONOPOLY, IN ANY MARKET, OCCURS NOT BECAUSE OF LIMITED SUPPLY OR AVAILABILITY OF A GIVEN PRODUCT, BUT MORE SO BECAUSE A GIVEN ENTITY CONTROLS THE MARKET WITH LITTLE OR NO CONCERN AS TO PRODUCT CHOICE."

Think of it this way: If I were able to convince you that the only source of breathable air was obtainable only from CleanAireCo, would it be unreasonable then to question why every air-breathing human purchases their supply of air from this company? Though unreasonable as it might seem, it is more unnerving that consideration is never given to the idea that there could quite possibly be an *alternate source* of breathable air. Likewise, as we will soon see, the faint cry of *that's absurd,* which might otherwise accompany one's conscience when one discovers that the practices integral to the concepts that support contemporary financial and/or monetary policies are only yet another

---

36   Alan Greenspan: Federal Reserve Chairman August 1987 through January 2006.

example of *Flat Earth Idolatry*-like notions. In other words, they are hopelessly biased and defiantly specious.

As we move through the discussion on monetary policy it would be of value to recall, periodically, *the two quotes which follow.* I believe it will make the subject that follows all the more entertaining:

> *"What is to become of the rumor*
> *that has lost its messenger?"*

And,

> *"A lie repeated often enough becomes the truth."*[37]

This would be a fine time to reacquaint ones self with the two quotes appearing at the end of the previous section entitled *Simple Economics*.

EXCHANGE OF VALUE

For as long as man has engaged in some form of commerce there has been a method or medium for exchanging value between or among parties of interest. Barter, as a basic form of exchange, is the typical and most common medium for basic commerce. Fundamentally, it is *the exchange of a good* or *service that possesses* inherent value for that of another's. Barter, much to the displeasure of the regulated economic system, is an example of this type of exchange. People barter in all sorts of ways, whether it be in the form of a favor for a favor, a side of beef for 50 yards of linen, or if you're an owner of a "timeshare," bartering

---

37   A quote often associated with the Nazi propaganda chief, Dr. Joseph Goebbels

one week per year at a Florida resort for another owner's interest in, let's say, Cancun, Mexico.

Now then, let us assume that the value of a one week per year timeshare located in Mexico is equal to the same time period for a resort in Florida. In this instance, the exchange is quite simple and equitable. Now then, if one happens to own a timeshare in Anchorage, Alaska, its exchange value may not be as valuable as a one week per year commitment in Honolulu, Hawaii. In this case, your one week in Anchorage may yield you only one night in Honolulu. In this instance we observe a disparity in value and therefore, an adjustment is necessary to balance the scales so that there is an equitable exchange between owners of value. In other words, the value of one is adjusted up/down so that the exchange of value becomes equal and thus, *Value Given, Value Received!* For purposes that will be more significant in the following section, let us refine the point one step further: A *presumed value* is exchanged for what is its equal in *presumed value*. The concept of *presumed value* is critical as it is the very foundation of money-value; this concept refines the presumption, or the pretense, used to establishes what *presumed value* measures. We will discuss this point in greater detail in a later segment of this chapter.

In our example of the timeshare, it is worth noting that there is no charge or fee (interest) associated with the establishing of this value. It would be absurd to think that the owner of the Hawaii timeshare (the more valuable) would surcharge the owner of the Alaskan timeshare for the use of this medium of exchange. To do so would, in effect, further lessen the value of the Alaska timeshare. An example of this *surcharge* is, as it might appear, illustrated as follows: The Hawaii owner offers the Alaskan owner one night in Honolulu in exchange for the seven nights in Alaska. However, for the privilege of being able to use this 7 to 1 ratio (the medium of exchange), the Alaskan owner must also include an additional (or eighth) night as part of the trade (the *surcharge*). In this instance, the Alaskan owner has but one week per year and if he wants that one night in Hawaii, what must he do? Well, in the barter system we've set up, he must exchange or pledge (perhaps even his next year's week in Alaska) an additional *thing* of value in order to acquire that one more (additional) *eighth* night.

Again, if the example is as clear as I intend it to be, one should clearly see that the exchange of the *value for value* (the seven nights in Alaska for the one night in Hawaii), represents the extent of the transaction. Also, and equally important, is that at the instant the exchange is made the *presumed value* of the Hawaiian timeshare, and likewise the Alaskan timeshare, has been established. The timeshares are what has been exchanged and nothing more. Adding to the process the concept of a *surcharge* is nothing more than *wealth consumption* which we've discussed in a previous section. This example illustrates an elementary introduction to the effect of interest/inflation, which requires more of one's resources to acquire a known or specific quantity of an item or service beyond its *presumed value*.

The *surcharge* concept also introduces, albeit on a very elementary level, the effects of *interest costs* as a component of *fiat monetary policy.* If the message appears to be a bit ambiguous, not to worry, it will become more precise in the section that will soon follow entitled *The Practice of Money.*

In order to build a solid foundation for the *monetary policy* discussion that follows, consider the following observations, particularly as they relate to the inclusion of the *surcharge* concept above. The *compound-*

ing effects of interest are wonderful from the vantage point of one's *savings* however, with respect to a nation's monetary policy (or if you are purchasing a home using a mortgage), particularly one that is based on *fiat* adaptations, the consequences are exponential in effect.

- The inclusion of the *surcharge* feature illustrates its policy flaw by attempt to extract or demand more from the system than what the *system* has been fueled to produce.

- The illustration shows how *wealth consumption* in excess of *wealth creation* produces a progressively greater loss, e.g., with each exchange for the Hawaii timeshare, the Alaskan timeshare owner surrenders a progressively greater number of future *rights* he has yet to *earn.* Sounds like *deficit spending!* Now then,

- We can see how quickly the *non-productive consumption* of *wealth* creates an economic imbalance in the system. Yes, the *surcharge* benefits the Hawaii owner to be sure. However, only for a time. Ultimately, the excess of *wealth consumption,* <u>supported by a temporary burst in demand masquerading as economic expansion,</u> is simply unsustainable without the regeneration of the system with additional *wealth creation.* As long as this practice of *all consuming* consumption persists, so will the cycle of *boom and bust!* It's *Simply Economics!*

The concept of exchanging *value for value* may seem so entirely elementary that I admit one might lose the significance of its simplicity, particularly when considering the tangled web of our contemporary economic structure. Yet, the *value for value* concept is, as I mentioned earlier, a *core fundamental* of sound *monetary policy* and one that has been ignored and lost to the fragmentation of cross purposes and *gray* logic.

Barter, as a practical function, works perfectly fine as long as there is a common exchange for establishing equitable value and parties of interest are reasonably close to one another. However, in an expanding economic environment, both financial and geographic, its limitations quickly become quite apparent. Surprisingly though, it is a far more common practice than one might realize. As I mentioned earlier in this section, the government rather frowns on a pervasive or an established practice of *barter,* largely as there is no effective means by which it might be taxed and as you know, we simply cannot tolerate too much prosperity.

> "PROSPERITY FEEDS THE FREE AND FERTILE MIND AND SO
> MAN REGARDS EVEN MORE SO, FREEDOM AND PROSPERITY.
> THIS FUELS THE ENVY AND CONTEMPT OF THE TYRANT
> AND SO HE MUST TAX TO SUPPRESS AND SUPPRESS SO THAT
> HE MAY TAX AND TAX AND THEN TAX YET AGAIN."

TRANSPORTABLE VALUE

To accommodate an expanding realm of commerce one can easily see that the barter system has its limitations. Man's expanding enterprise, as well as the notion of trading for goods and services that he may have as a product of his own industry (or scarcity of the same) for those of another, gave rise to the need for an *instrument of value.*[38] Not only an

---

38   Instrument of value (IOV): I use this term frequently to mean, simply, currency – currency in the form of paper money or coin, but not to the exclusion of historical incidents of other "IOV's."

instrument of value but one, expressed or identified as an *individual unit*, that can be easily recognized as being *of value* in a form expressing said individual *unit* or denomination. And of course, the fundamental requirement of this individual unit's being of value *is* that it must also be *transportable*.

This concept of a *transportable value* has been observed, in many forms, throughout history. An island nation might use shells or sharks' teeth, a Native American tribe might use seeds and yet another might use salt, precious gems or stones. All in their own unique environment, easily recognizable, readily identified by unit (a single seed, gem or stone) as having some measure of *presumed value* such that when combined together, one can increase the numbers of units and thereby increase their value to suit the demands of the transaction.

However, to be completely transportable, consideration had to be given to creating an individual unit capable of representing a *stored value* which can then be exchanged, at a later time, for the value of a good or service equal to the individual unit's stored value. Here, once again, we observe another seemingly anonymous custom that in the evolution of allegedly sophisticated monetary practices has faded into *gray*. I refer to this concept as the *instrument of value being evidence of a stored value*. We might also even more appropriately call it a *banked value*, which is particularly interesting in light of the origins of what we today, commonly refer to as a *Bank*.

The idea of creating an *instrument of stored value* became a matter of practical necessity. On any given day you may have a neighbor in need of a cartload of peat of which you happen to have an ample supply, yet he has nothing to offer that you find suitable for the balancing component of your exchange. Another may find himself laying stone for a Roman aqueduct and as a form of compensation he receives loaves of bread however, one can only eat so much bread before it succumbs and needless to say, a larder full of dry loaves of bread is not a particularly effective system for *banking value*. Necessity being the mother of invention required the creation of a transportable and functional instrument of *stored value*; accordingly, we see the appearance of coinage and paper money as early as 1000 B.C. It wouldn't be long before the solution creates yet another problem in search of yet another solution with *profit as its cause*. This would be, yet again, a wonderful time to reacquaint ones self with the quotes offered at the end of the section titled *Simple Economics*.

"MONEY HAS NOT ROOTS FROM WHICH TO DRAW FROM THE WELL OF EVIL. IT DOES, HOWEVER, TEND TO ATTRACT A RATHER CURIOUS PACK OF WOLVES!"

Before moving on to the next section, "Practice of Money," I need to refine a point for the reader that is most critical. It is the seminal point in all that follows. As I said earlier, *money or monetary policy is not at all complex. It is quite simply the creation and use of an instrument of value, by unit, that represents stored (or banked) value which is then used as a medium of exchange.* It is very important to grasp the simplicity of this premise as it will soon become abundantly clear why the U.S. (and world) financial system is in utter disarray and why continuing the monetary practices of the day *will yield accelerated and perpetual hardship*. Most importantly, it should be clear to all that these practices are wholly un-reconcilable with the ambitions of a free and just people, wherever it is they call home.

"Scenes are now to take place as will open the eyes of credulity
and of insanity itself, to the dangers of a paper medium
abandoned to the discretion of avarice and of swindlers."[39]

It is from this point on and throughout the remainder of this exercise that the image becomes clearer; the pagan gender of arrogance becomes visible and the message is made ever more compelling! In the end, there is only one choice, there are no options, there is no putting off to another day the course that will define and become our collective history! The issue of *monetary policy* must be resolved if we are to survive its errant practices whose effects have destroyed every country who dared tempt its excesses.

"IN THE MIDST OF THE TROUBLED MASSES THERE STANDS
A PIPER AND HE PLAYS THE CLEVER TONE OF AN EMPTY
PITCH SO CLEVERLY DISGUISED. YES HE PLAYS AND THEY
LISTEN, HE SMILES AS HE LEADS THEM FOR HE'S PLANNED
THEY'LL NOT KNOW BOTTOM 'TILL THEY'VE HIT!"

---

39   Thomas Jefferson: Excerpted from a letter written by Mr. Jefferson to Dr. Thomas Cooper, September 10, 1814. Key to the premise of his correspondence was his introduction to the subject "The crisis, then, of the abuses of banking is arrived."

The Practice of Money

ONCE WE ACCEPT THE NEED for this portable instrument of value (which from here on we'll simply refer to as *money* or *currency*) we then must resolve to settle two basic issues: (1.) Who will create *it?* And, (2.) What will be its *presumed value?* Throughout history we observe great conflict and economic turmoil arising out of these two very basic requirements and it is always a battle over *who* will control these two issues that will be at the heart of said conflagration. If we as a nation are to survive and prosper, I assure one and all that resolving to an appropriate outcome will require individuals of great courage and principle willing to wage battle if we are to emerge and recover from this political and economic quagmire.

In practical terms, the creation of currency, be it paper or coin, falls principally to either of two competing interests: *private* (banking institutions) or *public* (government treasury) *institutions*. The establishment of the currency's worth/value is then also left to these very same entities who by or through their own proprietary methods determine or prescribe a *presumed value* for the newly created currency. Pull out your paper currency or coinage, the *presumed value* is either pressed or printed on its *face*.

In developing a clear understanding of the practice of money, particularly from the point of origin or its creation, one must fully grasp that with these two competing models of currency creation, *private* vs. *public*, it is important to consider that one (private) is a *for-profit enterprise* and the other (public) is a *not for-profit system*.

To refine the point even further: The *for-profit* model *accumulates* wealth (not creating wealth mind you) by the *creation* and *use* of its currency, while the *not-for-profit* model *creates* currency not only as a means to facilitate its (the public's) commerce, but also as an evidentiary instrument that measures *stored* or *banked* wealth. This is a *very important* distinction between the two systems and a significant point of departure where *form* and *function* are concerned.

To fully understand the practice of these *two competing functions* I think it best to first present the foundation on which both of these two methods rest. So then, let us first pass through a discussion on:

PRESUMED VALUE

Whatever the individual *unit* (currency, salt, seed or precious stone or metal), there must first be an understanding of what the value of this *unit* represents. In short, what is the inherent or *stored value* of this *unit* as it relates to purchasing power so that when it is exchanged one receives equitable or *equal value* for the *unit(s)* one has surrendered? Example: The factory worker exchanges his value, presumably an eight-hour day, for an equal value, in currency, of what has been established as the dollar value of a day's work. The agreement on what this unit(s) value is then becomes the *presumed value*. The concept would appear in this way: A factory worker values an hour (a *unit* of exchange) of his work day at a rate of $25 per hour or $200 per day and so, in exchange for $200 (the employers *unit* of exchange), the worker exchanges an equitable amount (his *unit* of exchange) of his productive industry (8 hours) to his employer. Couldn't be more simple; *Value Given, Value Received.*

Historically this was achieved by using a *specie* or unit/currency that had intrinsic value, which is why so often throughout history, gold or silver was used in the minting of coins. The *presumed value* of these coins, thereby, was implied as evidenced by its unit's stored value. In its simplest form it would be explained thus: A gold/silver piece (coin) represented a volume of gold/silver equal to its face (*unit*) value, e.g., a $1 gold coin or a $.50 silver coin consisted of an equal measure of gold/silver. The structure of this type of monetary system requires a regimented system which maintains a *uniform measure of value* for the precious metal otherwise the treasury would constantly have to change the size or composition of its coinage. In actuality, one observes this occurrence with U.S. coins an example of which being the "penny" whose composition, historically, has been copper.

It then follows that the extent of the currency in circulation becomes dependent on the resources of the treasury to accumulate, in its reserves/ stores, gold or silver bullion. One can easily see, in this instance, how a fixed supply of gold or silver places a functional restraint on economic growth. An *expanding economic system* that is truly a *wealth creating* enterprise must also have a monetary system that expands with it. Referring once again to an earlier discussion, we can observe the soundness of this economic model. Applying the most rudimentary monetary policies, we can see how a *wealth creating economy*, in and on its own, creates and amasses an incredibly vibrant measure of *intrinsic value*. It is, by the way, the *only* means by which a nation, through its *wealth creating economy*, can amasses the gold/silver to create and support the presumed value of its currency. Again, the *only way*. However, what I am not suggesting is that a nation must only or can only have a vibrant *wealth creating economy* by amassing gold/silver stores as a measure of or mechanism for supporting the *presumed value* of its currency. More on this point in due course.

Conversely, we can also see how absent a *wealth creating* economy (such as we have currently), a nation's economic system will most assuredly collapse. The U.S. economy proves this point quite well: *wealth consumption in excess of wealth creation = economic suicide.* I would further argue that whatever appearances of wealth there may be occur only from the inertial or kinetic benefit (residual) of past wealth though whatever residue there might have been is now making its way through the predatory vacuum. This point will become even more apparent as we proceed through the remainder of this section.

> *"It would be best that our medium should be so*
> *proportioned to our produce, as to be on a par*
> *with that of the countries with which we trade,*
> *and whose medium is in a sound state."[40]*

At this point, I'll trust one will hold to the thought, at least for the time being, that *there is a direct connection between economic health and sound monetary policy.*

The matter of *presumed value* charts a rather curious course when applied to the creation of currency by way of a *private source.* As a point of order, the practice of establishing a *presumed value* for currency, in this instance, is seemingly the most effective way of accomplishing the task. However, lying just below the surface of this seemingly benign approach is one absolute truth:

---

40   Thomas Jefferson: Taken from a letter he penned to John W. Eppes, his son-in-law, then a congressmen and Chairman of the Ways and Means Committee. In this letter, among other issues, Jefferson's discourse was focused primarily on currency/banking and public debt.

"TO EXPECT ONE TO EXCHANGE A 'THING' OF VALUE FOR SOME 'THING' POSSESSING LITTLE OR NO VALUE SOON EXHAUSTS THE CYCLE OF EXCHANGE. TO SUGGEST THAT ONE SHOULD SERVES ONLY TO PROVE THE OUTCOME TO WIT, THAT WHICH FOLLOWS BEING MORE OF THE SAME, BECOMES INCREASINGLY WORTH LESS!"

This comment is intended to expose the soft underbelly of rogue monetary policy. Further, it illustrates the great risk of having no correlative value as a regimented component of a nation's currency. When the supply of currency, as it does in the U.S., exceeds the value of the economy's ability to support its *presumed value* (also known as "notional value"), which is the measure of its actual economic output, every unit of currency in excess of the economic output exponentially devalues the currency's *presumed value.* I will illustrate how this occurs in the section entitled "The Dangers of Fiat Money;" for now one will easily recognize one of the most conspicuous excesses: *Inflation.*

Recalling the *for-profit* model of the *private* banking structure, it stands to reason that one should not be surprised that parties having ownership interests in such an enterprise would want to insure a lucrative trade and it would be foolish to expect otherwise. Frankly, on a rather base level, I admire the genius of the private banking interests and their ability to lure the willing and compliant away from any semblance of reason and sound monetary practices. As with any nation who abdicates it sovereign wealth management process, the mere existence of a private central bank in control of any nation's monetary system is indicative of extremely persuasive influences at work. It is also an indication of how a people become vulnerable to the reckless monetary practices of a political system compromised to such a degree that they are either unable to or incapable of comprehending the dangers of these very practices.

As is the case in the U.S., the currency creation function is the express domain of the Federal Reserve. The Federal Reserve, though created by an act of Congress in 1913, is actually not a government agency and is, in fact, a completely private entity.[41] The process by which it creates money is surprisingly simple, it just prints it! The currency is then distributed to the *Fed's* various member banks and it migrates into the economic/financial system. Truly, that is all there is to it. For the privilege of using the Federal Reserve system, the federal government pledges "the good faith and credit" of the United States government, which includes all of its resources, as collateral evidenced by various *instruments* (debt) on which the government pays interest (to the Federal Reserve). Since 1913, every dollar spent by the U.S. government and every dollar in circulation was created in this way and orchestrated by this system.[42]

The term *fiat* is used to describe this type of currency creation; a currency with no intrinsic value, which then leads full circle to the idea of its *presumed value*. In a *fiat* money system, the *presumed value* is actually presumed to be worth the denomination printed on the paper note, also described as its *notional value*. Its purchasing power is largely based on whatever the market says it is at that time and as we can see by world currency fluctuations, this can mean any amount at any time, including *zero*. Again, the U.S. currency (actually a *Federal Reserve note*) possesses only the value the user believes it has and nothing more.

---

41 The reader may find it interesting to note that the Federal Reserve Act was passed by what appears to be very suspicious circumstances. The Congressional Record seems to imply that believing that the bill would not be brought to a vote until after the Christmas recess; many senators had left for the holidays without the Senate having formally adjourned. The bill was passed, with only three senators actually present by a procedural "unanimous consent" and then ultimately by "voice vote."

42 The only medium (or specie) created by the U.S. Treasury are coins.

To be fair to the Federal Reserve system, it does attempt to create support for the currency's *presumed value* by integrating the currency into *various mediums* thereby creating demand (support) for its value. The *Fed* is able to accomplish the *support* structure primarily as the dollar is the *world reserve currency* though the *Euro* (the common European currency), due to the dollar's declining value, has been gaining a more preferential standing though this is largely an orchestrated function of various central banks and market (currency) manipulations. A currency having the status of *reserve* is often the medium of value used in global/ international markets for the pricing of commodities (e.g. gold and oil). Conveniently, this status also *creates demand* for that very same *reserve currency* (the U.S. Dollar) and as coincidence would have it, this practice creates a extremely lucrative market for speculation known as *currency arbitrage*.

THE DANGERS OF FIAT MONEY

A *fiat money* system does offer convenience to an economic system. It serves the needs of an economy by providing a medium of exchange and it serves government's desire to spend with reckless abandon. In the day to day operations of one's industry, however, we take no notice of the price or cost this system imposes on our economic health. It appears and functions quietly until the day one discovers there is an insufficient amount of *nothing* to acquire *something*. Consider, if you will, the image equivalent to this quip being similar to that of a giant pine tree having become dinner for an army of wood-boring beetles. From the outside the tree appears quite substantial and robust even though it is only a shell of its former self. Translating this to the real world it appears this way: The government becomes encumbered *(pledged)* to the Federal Reserve from the debt it accumulates. In turn, the government, through the practices of unchecked legislative authority, encumbers the people's productive and economic value in order to *service* the mounting debt. In essence, the people become slaves to the government and the government (and its conscripted resources) become slaves to the Federal Reserve.

What follows is a quick summary of what I believe to be the primary weaknesses of this monetary/banking system:[43]

1. The debt assumed by the federal government through this process can *never* be repaid. Why? The repayment of the debt, assuming one could take this approach, would require the creation of more debt in order to pay off the existing debt, which in turn, would simply creates more debt, all of which serves to further devalue existing currency already in circulation.

2. The debt assumed by the federal government is attached with the requirement of periodic interest payments *(debt service)*. In order to make available sufficient funds for *servicing* the underlying debt and absent an increase in tax revenues, the process will therefore require the creation of additional debt (excluding, for the moment, the added debt simply to cover the requisite *debt servicing costs*). This not only further supports the statement in the preceding comment but also proves the fundamental danger of the *fiat* monetary system. In other words, the system constantly requires an ever-expanding debt model if for no other reason than to simply pay the accrued interest portions as they come due. The growth rate of both the debt and the accrued interest is exponential and which in

---

43   In this series of enumerated points I use the term *debt* to simplify the discussion. In practice, technically or in theory, to create or expand currency supplies, the *Fed* purchases Treasury Bills created by various security dealers. Federal *Debt* is evidenced by various types of *instruments*, e.g., "Bonds".

turn, makes resolving the debt load a fundamental and *mathematical impossibility*!

3. Accepting the two previous points as a foundation, the following should undoubtedly stir one's curiosity: Would the Federal Reserve accept, as payment for this debt, the very currency it creates? The answer should be fairly obvious which then begs a follow-up question: What does or would the Federal Reserve accept for payment? Contained with in the very provisions enabling the Federal Reserve is the answer: *Gold.* Which then leads me to a very stern and troubling observation: Is Fort Knox protecting what is purported to be the content of that facility or is it more likely that it is keeping the public from discovering the truth about what it does not own? At one time the single largest and justly accumulated (by the product of a nation's *wealth creating engine)* store of gold in history whose ownership is known only by those who possess it. What I am not suggesting, necessarily, is that there is no gold in Fort Knox. However, what I am considering is that what gold may actually be at this facility may not be owned by the U.S. Treasury and by extension, the People of The United States.

4. By or through the creation and/or the assumption of debt, the federal government knowingly or unknowingly pledges ALL of the resources of the United States government to the Federal Reserve. By extension, this also means any entity that uses the Federal Reserve Note and/or the Federal Reserve system. Can you think of one person or state, not to mention the federal government, that does not engage in the use of this currency or system? If you are interested in discovering the extent to which you are pledged as collateral, let me offer a simple exercise in which most people might participate: The next time you write a check for payment of your federal taxes (which you believe are being paid to the Internal Rev-

enue Service for the benefit of the United States government) and if by honest mistake, you were to write your check to the I.R.S., once the check is returned in your monthly bank statement, I urge you to inspect the back of the cancelled check and look at the *endorsement*. You will not only discover something quite interesting but you will also come to understand, quite possibly, why your senator or congressman refuse to overhaul the federal tax system.

5. A fiat money system survives only on an *ever expanding money supply model* which, consequently, requires perpetual inflation and deflationary cycles. Economic cycles of the *boom or bust* type are not the product of capitalism's economic engine; they are the result of a fiat monetary system which benefits immensely from the occurrence and persistence of these cycles. In practical terms, inflation *is* the silent killer-tax syphoning off resources and encumbering the people's wealth in perpetuity. This perpetual economic caste system occurs in a *fiat* monetary process for the same reasons explained in reference "2." above: The system, if only from the vantage point of sustainability, is a *mathematical impossibility*. For the American household, the tangible effects of this systemic *impossibility* occur for the simple reason that *effective wages* can never keep pace with the consequential burden of inflation. This reality, of course, is the cause of the massive explosion of consumer debt. In other words, an individual has only one reason to assume the burden of debt, whether it be for basic necessities or for a commodity beyond basic subsistence levels: *Insufficient income or purchasing power.* As we can see in our present day mortgage crisis, this *inflationary* and *deflationary (boom and bust) cycle* is playing out before our very eyes. Inflationary pressures caused by errant monetary policy *trigger the illusion of wealth creation,* one example of which is rising home values. The property owner borrows money

THE PRACTICE OF MONEY

(leveraging his home) to be used to subsidize the cost of living not being met by household income. The inflationary cycle ultimately reaches an unsustainable point and the reverse deflationary cycle takes over. *The Economy contracts, the system moves in and acquires more of what it already (foreclosures and repossessions) has and the people are left with even less than they had before.* Make no mistake, these cycles are planned and practiced. The stage is then set for the next cycle to begin again and as the government has pledged your productive capacity as collateral for the debt it assumes, *you are trapped.* With nowhere to turn, you are forced to play along and endure your quiet desperation.

6. A *fiat* money system effectively makes government a *spend-o-holic* and as we now know, government is never willing to address a mistake in policy or action. The nature of the political animal is to use guile to camouflage its indiscretions, particularly those relating to monetary policy or fiscal discipline. The method of choice is to always deflect the public's attention by simply doing more of the same. The logic seems to be: *As long as I give you more of what you want, your free health care, your paid-for retirement, your farm subsidies, your free prescription drug plan, your collective bargaining structure, this handout or that handout or for that matter, whatever I tell you or define for you as being that which you should want, you'll accept more of it and you, the over-fed lap dog, will never question how the government provides it or how it plans to pay for it.* Well, in the fiat money system, this scurrilous practice is easily accomodated. The tragedy, the true tragedy, is that the politician really doesn't want to know of the poison he offers; he simply likes having the ability to do so and like you, it couldn't matter less what is surrendered for what is presumed to have been gained. I am of the opinion that

there is something gravely wrong with this ethos and its practice. And,

7. Always be aware that in a *fiat* money system wealth is accumulated only by the willing transfer of wealth *from* the nation that is persuaded it cannot exist without the *system* which, to stress the point once again, benefits from this process occurring. I of course believe that not only can we exist without a *fiat* money system but that if we are to give meaning to the ideals of true freedom and true justice then we cannot live with it. The *fiat* money system operates strictly on a *for-profit* model and its profits are created and accumulated by commanding wealth through enforced use of its system. This system has no sense of patriotic duty or national resolve, it exists only to evolve and in so doing it persists not by creating wealth but from amassing wealth and the political and economic influence that accompanies the same.[44]

"THE DAWN HAS COME TO A DAY WHERE WE
NEITHER OWN THE PRODUCT OF OUR EFFORTS NOR
THE ABILITY TO CLAIM THAT WE SHOULD!"

Again, from the vantage point of a businessman who is by his very nature a *for-profit* proponent, I have no issue with the concept as a theoretical advantage. In the practice of any of my business interests, for example as a land developer, I readily admit I could amass an amazing fortune if I could command that anyone, anywhere, who has need for a tract of land to build a home, a factory, a school, etc., could only do so (as I would control all undeveloped land) by acquiring the land from me; a fabulously self-serving and monopolistic idea! Clearly this

---

44 The reader should not confuse these statements of *monetary policy* with the practice of *lending* money. This discussion relates solely to the creation of money through the creation of debt.

can't be and so, regardless of how one might favor the idea, there is a profound conflict with this notion in application. I am suggesting that once ample consideration is given to the subject, I believe any reasonable person will arrive at the same conclusion. This leads to my final comments, for now, on the matter.

Fiat money policies appear to work in expansive economic environments where wealth creation is occurring. An example of this would be the post-WWII era with the expansion and explosion of baby boomers. The advent of consumerism triggered an economic cycle which evolved to produce various products in order to fill the exploding demand fueled further by product creativity and productive capacity. This economic period of true wealth creation (also a period with the lowest level of foreign imports) is often used as a source for both *macro* and *micro economic* study supporting the contrivances of *Keynesian* economic theory and as well misused as a corroborating mechanism supporting both *fiat monetary policy* and *deficit spending*. However, there are serious deficiencies in using these assertions in correlating a causal relationship between theoretical and practical economic realities. Consider the following points representative and reflective of our discussions in the previous section titled *Simple Economics*.

The economic resurgence of post-WWII America is more likely a response to sociological conditions and not government stimulus programs. The economic engine is driven from the bottom up and not the top down; it is purely *organic* and never contrived. This precisely explains why Roosevelt's *New Deal* programs were a disaster and why every government attempt, including the current administration's, will fail miserably and do so for one critical reason: They are *wealth consuming*. This observation is wholly consistent with the *native economy* concepts provided earlier.

The fiat monetary policy concepts and practices were not exposed to their greatest risks/faults until well in to the Vietnam era. The *wealth creation* vs. *wealth consumption* model is proven by observing the post-WWII era features where sufficient net *wealth creation* was sufficient to subsidize the demands of government until such time as government borrowing (debt funded spending) placed unsustainable demands upon the economic system and/or cycle and this burden continues to this day. To be clear, I am deliberately referring to, but not to the exclusion of other actions equally culpable, the explosion of unfunded and unregulated government spending for the many entitlement programs all of which are a direct and specific example of the consequences associated with disturbing the *operational parameters* of a *functional economic system.*

Further, when these consequential excesses do, as they have, occur the glaring deficiencies of the *fiat* money system, absent real economic productivity, begin to expose its systemic and operational flaws. The most conspicuous of these (flaws) is evidenced by the causal relationship between inflation and the government's insatiable appetite for *debt spending* necessitated by an ever expanding spending regiment. We are all saturated with the tangible consequences which are evidenced by the economic and financial quagmire we observe and endure at the present time. Rest assured, with no deliberate and fundamental restructuring, the social, political and economic environment will continue to degrade.

To summarize this point, let us then resolve to this fundamental truth as it relates to fiat monetary policy: Absent functional *wealth creation* practice and cycles, the economic system then requires *perpetual inflationary monetary policy* as a substitute for the absence of true *wealth cre-*

ation's beneficial effects. In turn, this practice accelerates inflation and the extraction of wealth from the economy as the result of government spending, debt accumulation and debt servicing requirements. The effects of these practices indiscriminately migrate across the spectrum to impose the very same virus upon both the private business and household sectors of the economy. In reality, this practice both siphons *wealth* out of the economy that would otherwise be used for productive *wealth creation* purposes and institutionalizes an actual systematic aversion to the *wealth creation process.*

"REST ASSURED THAT IF YOU ARE A BELIEVER IN REINCARNATION, THE DEBT WILL STILL BE HERE WHEN YOU RETURN! I PROMISE!"

A *fiat* money system can be made to work although the methods employed to affect its use have frequently been criticized as being a form of nostrum.[45] The opponents are usually the advocates, or their representatives, of the *for-profit* banking approach, which, frankly, should come as no surprise. As I've studied monetary policy over the years, I have come to the simple conclusion that *monetary practices of the day serve no other purpose than to extract and redirect value from an economic system.* As it is, I can see no beneficial effect of making a *non-vested* interest the ultimate authority of this or any nation's financial or economic future, not to mention the adverse influences that prowl the arteries of government. Rest assured though, this system will not willingly surrender its influences. If one finds an interest in American history, I would suggest a visit with the historical events surrounding the War of 1812 as well as President Andrew Jackson's battles with various banking interests; I believe one's inquiry will be well worth the effort and the discovery quite revealing.

---

45   Nostrum, as I use it here, is simply another way of saying *quack medicine.*

Consider this: If, as is the case, the Federal Reserve can simply print money, why then can the U.S. Treasury not do the same? If the *good faith and credit* of the United States government is sufficient for the *Fed* and the end-users of the system, it would seem to me little difference should one simply eliminate the middleman. Perhaps I should approach the query in this way: If the *presumed value* of the currency is based on the *good faith and credit* of the United States government, what would be the difference if the currency stated *U.S. Treasury Note* rather than *Federal Reserve Note?* The collateral is still the same; the truth of the matter is there is no difference.

In colonial America, and at various times until the creation of the Federal Reserve, there were several instances where government (U.S. Treasury) adhered to its sovereign duty of sound monetary discipline and the system worked quite well.

> *"That is simple. In the colonies we issue our own money.*
> *It is called Colonial Script. We issue it in proper pro-*
> *portion to the demands of trade and industry to make*
> *the products pass easily from the producers to the*
> *consumers. In this manner, creating for ourselves our*
> *own paper money, we control its purchasing power,*
> *and we have no interest to pay to no one."*[46]

To his credit, Abraham Lincoln discovered, when in search of the necessary resources to fund the Civil War, that the Constitution enabled him to avoid the *usurious rates* of the bankers. He simply printed "greenbacks," which were guaranteed by the government and these remained in circulation for years despite the efforts of bankers to

---

46   Benjamin Franklin (1763): His response to an inquiry by the Bank of England as to the cause of the colony's prosperity.

assert that these *notes* were worthless. By the way, on your next visit to Washington D.C. I recommend standing on the steps of the Lincoln Memorial and, depending on the seasonal foliage, if one were to direct their view along the course of *Henry Bacon Drive* the facade of the Federal Reserve can be seen. I often muse over the subtle irony as to the placement of these two national ornaments particularly as to their respective deference to our *national ideals*. Clearly, they are polar opposites.

The history of banking in the United States is littered with evidence of converging interests. The existing *fiat* money system exists not because it is *sound policy* but because the interests that benefit from its practice were simply better at crafting a strategy insuring its adoption and absent a vigilant opposition, that is precisely what happened. I'm of the opinion we can do better; I'm of the belief that we will have to!

> *"Whosoever controls the volume of money in any country is*
> *absolute master of all industry and commerce...*
> *And when you realize that the entire system is very*
> *easily controlled, one way or another, by a few powerful*
> *men at the top, you will not have to be told how*
> *periods of inflation and depression originate."*[47]

PROSPECTS FOR THE FUTURE

What I'm suggesting is a *hybrid* monetary system. One that simply combines many of the same practices of the current system without the *systemic casualties* we've come to endure. It will require courage and dis-

---

47   President James Garfield, circa 1881.

cipline which have, admittedly, become foreign concepts, but mostly it will require vigilance. Yes, there will be objections and they will all come from the proponents of the existing system who will endlessly chronicle the problems with this developed proposal, however none will truly be able to formulate a sound objection to the value and clarity of its systemically pure design and fundamentals. Here are a few of what might be offered as the idea's most significant problems:

1. Under this alternate fiat money system, as the U.S. Treasury would be printing the currency, it would serve no purpose to charge itself interest. If there is no need to pay interest to oneself then the *mathematical impossibility* issue is eliminated and thereby, inflationary/deflationary spirals.

2. Under this alternate system, as there is no need to create an encumbrance to a private entity, there would be no need to have collateral, which, in turn, eliminates government debt and if there is no collateral/debt, there is no control. Now then, having removed the devices of control, the overbite of fear is no longer a medium of influence.

3. Under this alternate system, the government might then observe the injustice of the current tax system, and its *wealth consuming* effects moving diligently toward restoring reason and fiscal discipline to the practice of funding government.

4. Under the alternate system, there would be no need to expand the global use of the currency to further command the application of the *for-profit* model. The U.S. Treasury Note would then be seen as an instrument of *value* based solely on the *wealth creating* economic engine's productive capacity. It then follows that to maintain and foster the strength of the currency's *presumed value,* the government would then see the merit of suspending legislation that

strips the *wealth creating* economic engine's ability to, you guessed it, be a *wealth creating* economic engine. The government might very well understand that it is in the best interests of a *free and just* people to rescind all legislation that prohibits or interferes with this ambition.

5. In this alternate system, inflation would be systemically controlled as the currency in circulation would be *tied* directly to the *wealth creating* capacity and not the *borrowing capacity* of the economic system. Thus merit, based on the pride of performance, may yet return as a valuable ethic and creative genius may yet become a valuable and coveted commodity.

6. In this alternate system, the *wealth created* will be sufficient to more than adequately fund the needs not only of the people, but the government as well. The concept of *self-reliance* will then not seem an impossibility and the illusion of benevolent government will be seen for the intrusion that it is. This is because true *wealth creation* works from the *bottom up* and not the *top down,* which, heretofore, has been seen as purely an anecdotal metaphor.

7. In this alternate system, the economic approach the economic system (on its own) becomes self-reliant and self-regulating; not by enforcement but out of necessity. This process occurs organically only in conjunction with a government willing to repel *coercive legislative* practices and let stand the *rule of law* to adjudicate, as it should, abuses.

8. In this alternate approach, the merits of the system will be self-evident. Nations wanting to trade with this country will do so as this country will no longer *practice predatory monetary* policies and our economic strengths will possess an estimable quality, as they once did. We will promote only *value for value* trading practices as long

as they are not detrimental to our sovereign interests. Our *economic interests* will no longer be secured at or by the point of a gun but by the strength of our economic system and our national character!

9. In this alternate system, having reclaimed our national stores of precious metals, the nation will once again be able to transact in a stable global economy, as all trading between nations of economic interest will occur only in or by a *value for value* principle, which will be either in *commodity* or in *bullion* or a combination of the two. This intermediary function would be a fine task for the International Monetary Fund (IMF) which might simply be repurposed as the *International Monetary Settlement Agency* where all international transactions are settled and/or arbitrated. Instead of persisting only as a meddling monetary black hole of antagonism, the United Nations (of which the IMF is a part) will also be repurposed as an international conglomeration of nations whose representatives administer their respective country's international commerce and where economic disputes, if any, are arbitrated.

These are but a few of the *problems* generated by a suitable alternative to the private *fiat* monetary system. Yes, of course I am being a bit sardonic, or, as it were, *tongue and cheek*. However if you must know, this approach *(alternate system)* is not at all absurd or unheard of as much of this proposed *hybrid* monetary system was a very common practice long before the *fractional reserve banking* concept and its offshoot, *fiat* money systems, became the norm. It is and was proven to be a functional and efficient system.

No, the *real problem* with this approach is not its structure; the problem *is that the private banking system will loose its ability to profit and its coercive influences.* The threat of this loss will make a few very wealthy and influential people extremely troubled and as I mentioned earlier, I assure you they will not surrender their influence willingly. If you are familiar with the Frank Capra movie, *It's a Wonderful Life*, then you will no doubt be familiar with *Mr. Potter*, the banker. Well, think of a room full of *Mr. Potters* and the image will perfect the message intended.

Here is a brief review of how this concept might function: The Federal Reserve, possibly, could continue to exist; however, it will be relegated to the function of a *national banking system manager* representing, though contained by absolute and precise provisions, *only* the U.S. Treasury (government) and nothing or no one else. It will simply be identified as the U.S. Federal Banking System (USFBS) and will be a department of the U.S. Treasury with specifically defined administrative capabilities. The U.S. Treasury will have to adopt a *procurement function* component as part of the restoration of gold/silver bullion however, this should be a reasonably manageable process and relevant only to the extent of expanding demands (as required) of global trade. If, as our past success would indicate, the promise of economic proficiency is recaptured, this nation should have no challenge in accumulating excess *stores*.

The USFBS will be managed by a board of nine governors who will be drawn from nine newly-developed regions. Each region will, through an electoral process, select its region's USFBS governor from a pool composed of duly elected state treasurers from each state of the respective region. A USFBS governor will serve for a maximum of three years including a not-to-exceed cumulative lifetime term of no more than six years. The USFBS permanent operational staff will be rotating and drawn from appropriately schooled personnel from the private sector or from other federal and/or state agencies. Their terms will be three years; however, in no event, shall their lifetime service exceed six years. No candidate shall be drawn from the private banking/financial industry or be a former or past employee of the U.S. Treasury or any federally elected office.

The legislative branch of the federal government, other than the requisite enabling legislation, will be barred from legislative action, save for those actions that are ratified by no less than three-quarters of the states. The framers of the Constitution intended the bicameral[48] form of government to limit or control collusion of dominant interests, accordingly, a rigid structure for a *national monetary system* should be considered for the very same reasons. I believe Mr. Jefferson would be very pleased! In 1798, having observed the various battles over government spending as well as the questionable affairs of, as he put it, "the banking influences," he realized that the Constitution had not fully addressed the issue and structure of monetary policy. With consideration to the era and these issues, his statement, as follows, animates his foresight quite well:

> *"I wish it were possible to obtain a single amendment to our Constitution - taking from the federal government their power of borrowing."*

Returning to our *hybrid* discussion and by way of refining the same, consider that the only other primary difference will be in the structuring of currency creation and policy practices. There will be ample opportunity for private banking interests, as well as existing financial markets, which will and can operate just as they do now, including

---

48   Bicameral refers to two distinct legislative bodies. In the U.S. this design is identified by the *Senate* and the *House of Representatives*. Although, technically, all are congressmen/congresswomen, conventional /practice dictates that this term is associated with members of the *House* (the *Lower House*) and senator for the Senate (the *Upper House*).

their practice of *fractional reserve banking.*[49] They will, however, have to operate on sound financial principals as there will no longer be the endless supply of *bailout* money from the Federal Reserve and the protection its political influence acquires. Their functions and practices, like those of every other American, will simply have to conform to national standards as will all lending practices. Their profits, as they should, will be the product of their industry as will be their losses. *The goal, it must be remembered, is to develop a functional monetary system –* that is conducive to a *wealth creating and sustaining* economic system and not the opposite. It should be obvious to any observer that the system, as it presently exits, is and has been, completely destructive.

A few final points on the subject: The *debt load* and *for-profit* bias components of the existing system will need to be eliminated as will all of the debt created by the Federal Reserve. This idea will likely be perceived and labeled as an economic apocalypse; however, I would simply refer the concerned back to the discussion on the manner in which the debt and currency are created in the first place. In any event, how can the outcome be possibly any worse than it already is or will become should the policy or practice of choice be more of the same? It is *only* a debt instrument (a "Federal Reserve Note") completely manufactured and created by a private enterprise from absolutely nothing, secured by *everything* of value. All that is being, or should be done is to eliminate the debt instrument. The good news is that any value on which this now-extinct debt is secured still remains long after the dead tissue has been excised.

A quick *side bar:* There is no Constitutional authority for the current system. Shame, once again, on the Supreme Court for not having the

---

49 Fractional reserve banking is the practice whereby banks lend out money based on their reserves, i.e. deposits, on hand. Often, presently, the ratio is 10:1, or lending $10 for every $1 on reserve.

courage to express its authority on behalf of the People it is charged to serve!

I persist on this point with the intent of driving home the simplicity of the cure. Yes, there will be financial chaos the world over, but the chaos will be confined to the industry that benefits from the present system, despite what you will be told. The commerce of economy, which I have defined as the *organic* or *native economy*, will continue to exist as the *motive force* which drives demand perpetually fueling a functional and vibrant economic cycle. So long as man populates the planet, he will intuitively purpose the means and motives for the entire economic event to occur. In this, there will be no change. The roles of government and business will simply be restored to being as they should: the guardian of The People's rights and the providers of goods and services for value in exchange for equal value. Not, as it presently is, the government as the guardian and advocate of interests adverse to those of The People!

Implicit in any functional system is the distinction of *role and purpose* as well as an understanding of and absolute alliance with there respective objectives. There is a distinct *role and purpose* for government as well as for business. There is also a distinct *role and purpose* for the mechanisms of a *nation's monetary policy* and system. It is a grave mistake to believe that these distinct objectives trend toward a moral and just cause and it is for this reason their select domains must be deliberately defined, refined and enforced all the while possessing an implicit and unilateral prohibition applicable to all; violation brings consequence which is assured, absolute, punitive and unavoidable. The *hybrid* model we've just reviewed tenders a great many opportunities for restoring fiscal discipline and sanity. Moreover, it is *practical, rational, balanced and sustainable* all of which must be mandatory components of any discussing on the topic of *Monetary Policy* and the *Practice of Money.*

An Adult Conversation

LET US ENGAGE in an adult conversation for one moment. Appling any basic principle of finance to the balance sheet of the U.S. economy/government, one will have no choice but to conclude that the U.S. is and has been, for several decades, financially bankrupt. The economic resources of this country are but a fraction of the mounting debt presently secured by the so-called "good faith and credit" of the United States and there is *absolutely no hope* of this debt ever being settled and that is an incontrovertible truth.[50, 51] If we add to this massive debt-load the unfunded benefits promised by benevolent government, the already bleak prospects for economic solvency become nothing less than a cosmic black hole.

In effect, what the government has done, not unlike a person seeking capital infusion to fund a dying business, is to have *collateralized the productive capacity* of the American economic engine in order to fund its habitual spending. Whereas a financial cure might otherwise be resolved by productive capacity, our greater crisis is the lifeless remains of a national economic engine that it has been packed up and shipped *off-shore*. However, the government continues its reckless ways and this, my dear friends, is just another incontrovertible truth. The *fiat* money

---

50   The current debt (Federal) @ 4/9/09, per the U.S. Treasury is $11 trillion and estimated to increase by $4 trillion in the current fiscal year alone. This estimate does not include, State and Local Government Debt ($3.5 Trillion), Federal Reserve Global "float" estimated to be $6.8 Trillion ("Fed" and BIS websites), private debt nor the estimated $100 trillion unfunded Medicaid/Medicare and Social Security demands. It is estimated these alone add $1 trillion per year to the aggregate unfunded amount. This number does not include the *debt service costs* or the incalculable cost of benefits generated by a Nationalized Healthcare system.

51   Not to mention the unresolved issue of "derivatives" and their numerous variants. The *Bank of International Settlements* in Basil, Switzerland estimates this total to be $1,144 trillion!

concept is not unlike the U.S. Federal Government; it has knowingly promised an outcome that it simply cannot or ever hope to deliver! This too, is an absolute truth!

> "WHAT GOVERNMENT HAS DONE, BY SUBMITTING TO THE GLOBAL MONETARY MYTH, IS TO HAVE RELEASED A SWARM OF LOCUSTS ONTO THE ECONOMIC LANDSCAPE OF THE GLOBE. THE PEOPLE, SIMPLY IN ORDER TO SURVIVE, HAVE UNKNOWINGLY BECOME ACCOMPLICES AND ARE LARGELY IGNORANT OF THE FORCED SUBMISSION AND ADOPTION OF THESE PREDATORY PRACTICES."

To the observing eye of any rational person clearly the national debt levels are unsustainable and for all practical purposes, *unserviceable*. The debt-levels (*see footnote #50*), in dollar denominations are so grotesquely unmanageable that if one were to project the current *productive capacity* of the U.S. Economy which I calculate to be to be approximately $3.5 Trillion annually (manufacturing, agriculture and mine output components of the U.S. Economy for 2009), it would take thirty-seven years to extinguish the debt and this estimate does not take in to account *debt-service* costs or the massive *derivative risks* that as yet remain unresolved.

Now then, to enhance the illustration further let me offer one more example of how extreme these debt levels have become: For fiscal year 2009 the U.S. Government reports that the total U.S. Household income was estimated to be $7.8 Trillion. If every household in the United States applied there total income toward the settling of the current debt-load it would require no less than sixteen years to eliminate this nation's debt-burden. Again, this estimate does not address *debt-service* costs or the outstanding *derivative risk* and assumes of course that the government suspends its preference for debt-funded spending and there is no further decline in household income.

The truth of the matter is that when considering the current government spending trends along with the effects of continued decline in domestic economic *wealth creating processes,* there is truly only one feasible alternative:

The U.S. Treasury will simply accumulate all of the Federal Reserve Notes in circulation and return them to their maker (The Federal Reserve Member Banks) replacing these with what will be a new U.S. government currency. Now then, what of the balance of the debt that is held by foreign central banks?[52] Well, there's an easy solution to this as well: As the current practice is simply that of central banks trading *fiat currency* for another central bank's *fiat currency* (all of which has the same fundamental policy of *presumed value*), they can simply exchange currencies. Nothing for nothing, as it were. I am aware that this approach may seem erratic and unrefined however the fact remains that spiraling inflation always accompanies *fiat monetary practices* so rest assured that nuclear devaluation of *sovereign currency* is inevitable. In the end, for holders of currency, the outcome is going to be the same either way.

For those who might favor the *Feds quantitative-easing* approach to *debt-remediation* let me express my sentiments this way: Creating new debt to settle existing debt, otherwise known as *monetizing,* is the very practice that is largely to blame for the current financial cataclysm this country faces and to tease the environment further with these methods is to only accelerate the inevitable collapse.

---

52 Foreign central banks: It is so very important to be aware that these *banks* are the very same (type) as the Federal Reserve. They are also private entities operating, in most cases, identical to that of the *Fed.*

The Outcome and Psychology
of Monetary Conquest

THE MOST COMMON OBJECTION, as mentioned previously, will likely revolve around a manufactured anxiety/fear on this issue which will characterize the new system as somehow predatory or protectionist. However, the truth of the matter is this: The value of this *debt* has already been made increasingly worthless due in large part to the *effects of inflation*. Regardless, the facts are undeniable, as under the current system the debt can never be repaid and the central (private) banks know and understand this. Therefore, as to the government debt held by the Federal Reserve, which is estimated to be 52%[53] of the total, I suggest we simply accelerate the inevitable.

We've been told for years not to worry about the government debt. If this, as it has been explained, is debt we owe to ourselves then it would follow that no U.S. citizen will mind if it disappears. This then simply leaves the balance of approximately 48% of the remaining global U.S. debt held by foreign (central) banks, private pension funds or investors and so on. This debt can be handled in either, or both, of the following manners: (1) *Inter* and *intra* bank (foreign or domestic) holdings will simply have to disappear. The *interests* have profited handsomely from the present structure for the better part of three-quarters of a century and the financial costs to the American people are immeasurable; they have, in my opinion, been sufficiently compensated. These *interests* can

---

53   The source of this estimate is a blend of Federal Reserve and U.S. Treasury sourced information. Due to the nimble nature of both these entities, precision was not obtainable.

settle amongst themselves using the gold/silver stores they retain once they've returned the bullion that rightfully belongs to the treasury of the respective nations from which it was obtained. (2) The debt in the hands of *foreign interests* (the value of which, as we can see, is spiraling downward on its own due to global market forces) other than central banks, will be given a declining redemption value structured over a period of five years at the conclusion of which it will become worthless; this will have occurred inevitably under current practices due to *debt monetizing*[54] practices. (3) Once the U.S. gold and silver bullion is restored, a uniform standard of value is established on a per ounce of gold/silver basis, which will be used by the *new* IMF in valuing each nation state's gold/silver stores used exclusively for settling of international currency exchange valuation and commerce. And, (4.) Any non-government pension (private), domestic or foreign, will be given 70% redemption value for a period of no more than 12 months post conversion date with a similar declining redemption value also structured over a remaining four year period.

I see no reason why this system cannot function well for any nation, particularly if that nation chooses to transact in the global marketplace. Frankly, I am of the opinion that we, as a nation, are on the verge of a planned economic and monetary conversion similar to that of European Union, albeit one that is more invasive and global in scope and scale; in truth, much of this conversion has already taken place. The IMF[55] is already making moves in this direction, the cover story for this being the suggestion that Russia and China are urging the replacement of the U.S. dollar as the world reserve currency.

---

54   Debt Monetizing: in its simplest and most barren form it is simply the creation of new debt to payoff or replace old debt. It is the erudite version of *kiting*.

55   The IMF, International Monetary Fund, has the ability to create what is known as a special drawing right *(SDR)* which, though technically not a currency, is more of a *claim* on or of a group of currencies on which its value, the *SDR* is based.

What Russia and China may not know, assuming the intent is simply not a well crafted ruse, is that they are playing right in to the hands of the IMF as the handmaiden of the *Fed,* the consequences of which will only serve to further tighten the grip of *global monetary policy.* Regardless, this should be seen as nothing but more of the same *smoke and mirror* monetary practices that have and will continue to devastate and plunder the economic resources of a sovereign nation and its people. Rest assured that those who orchestrate the *Fed's* actions are bright and persuasive people who have, for hundreds of years, honed the practice of *economic conquest.* The system has learned that arrogant and divisive politicians are easily controlled simply by the practice of feeding their egos and their vices. Likewise, the system is not at all concerned about *The People.* Why? They know the politicians will deliver you with ease and, if necessary, at the point of a gun!

Extreme observation? No, sadly, it is only the imprint of history's film projecting itself once again! Either way, it is this understanding that surreptitiously gives the existing system its *hold* and I make this promise: The remedy for the economic chaos (which is only just beginning) will be billed as being your salvation and your sentiments on the subject will be engineered so that you will submit to believing that it is precisely that; your salvation. For any person with a perspective similar to my own, yours will be the dubious distinction of simply being labeled a *quack.* It will be sold as your punishment for years of excess and entitlement, your penance for your productive capitalist ways or any other possible variant in the extreme. Regardless of the crafting of the message, it will be the means by which the idea of *globalism* will be secured.

A *fiat* money system survives for a time only with the *persistent creep of inflation*. It persists by an ever-expanding and willing field of participants whose wealth and productivity is the object of predation. The coded message of this is the *We are making the world safe for democracy* and *economic interest* speech so often used to commit not only our financial resources but our most precious resource of all, human lives.

Americans have been told *cheap labor* (foreign) has been the gift that has provided our nation's emancipation from the squalor of an industrial powerhouse to the ascendant bliss of a *service-based economy*. Viewing our native economic wasteland, clearly this is not an accurate representation. What it is *is* the unholy marriage of unfettered monetary/business interests and practices expanding its fields of influence aided by a willing and compliant government; all of which is sold to the public by way of a *manufactured crisis*.

What type of *crisis?* Feel free to take your pick from the veritable cornucopia of media-locusts willing to fill the void of conscious thought, each strategically targeted to overwhelm your reason by attacking your most vulnerable component. Many of the more common will appear quite familiar: Oil shortage, financial markets, food shortage, water shortage, power shortages, pandemics, global cooling, global warming, terrorism[56], human rights and so on and so on!

What is the price? Your freedom, *always* the price is *freedom!*

I readily admit that some of these statements may appear as the miscellaneous ramblings of an extreme quisling. By way of addressing this

---

56   I'm not suggesting that terrorism is necessarily a *manufactured crisis*. I do find it interesting that much is done identifying it and much is done to cannibalize American's personal freedoms and liberties, but little is done to eliminate the problem. There's a reason the subject remains so conspicuously ambiguous.

perspective, I submit the following observations: Consider how easily the economic capacity of Germany was surrendered to the *E.U.* with not a whimper. How effectively the *Reds* railroaded the hearty Russian people into Communist submission. How easily the Jews and non-conformist Christians were marshaled into the concentration camps of Nazi Germany. Observe how easily the freedoms of the American People were vaporized by the intrusive and draconian policies proffered by the deceptively labeled *Patriot Act*. I predict the time is not far off when one will no longer be able to transit the United States absent a locator device of some form. After all, if you are an otherwise law abiding citizen, what possibly do you have to fear from the Authorities? Interesting question, particularly when one considers that it is the criminal who avoids detection or, in the case of the *9/11*, are simply ignored! Consider further how the U.S. industrial capacity has been looted with the *wink and nod* of the U.S. Congress who willingly and ruthlessly surrendered your economic capacity to the design prescribed by the WTO/GATT/NAFTA/CAFTA *treaties* which, by the way, few politicians bothered to read!

For any individual who constructively reviews the ruminations of the day, is there any open debate as to *why* the U.S. government continues to be unwilling to secure our national identity by enforcing a structured and measured immigration policy? What possible reason could there be, particularly in the case of a southwestern border state, for an elected official not to insist on strict border enforcement?

The American public is regularly silenced or programmed by a well-orchestrated media push along with the obsequious politicians who want you to believe you've been elevated to the refinement of a more productive *serviced-based* economy, or the ruse of *we are a nation of immigrants* or *we are securing our freedoms by surrendering our liberties* being just a few of the prearranged *orders of the day.* I shudder to think of the benign explanation my congressmen would offer for this sellout. How might one rationally believe that an economy can prosper by feeding on itself. Kindly repeat after me: *A willing and compliant government.*

It is quite possible that it has been only the natural alliance of human desire and its native genius that has kept the system from complete collapse. The pure force of will of a People intuitively driving the irreversible machine of progress all orchestrated by our native desire and genius the composition of which is progenerative by design. I think of a thoroughbred trapped in the confines of the starting gate, all the while understanding that its native form and purpose is to be free, to run, to be in motion and as such it is in constant struggle with *the forces* that would otherwise confine it. Sooner or later, if the horse is not free to do what it naturally does, fatigue and lethargy will abide and the fracturing of its spirit will soon follow. This statement characterizes the image of what I have previously referred to as the *native economy!* It also expresses its vulnerabilities.

In my lifetime I've seen, in many ways, the product of the human spirit and genius the likes of which haven taken my breath away. I have come to believe that our struggle is not with what's outside of us but more so with our internal conflicts. And though there is much to say on this subject I will simply summarize my thoughts in this way:

"WE STRUGGLE NOT BECAUSE OF OPPRESSION; WE STRUGGLE
DUE TO A CRISIS OF CONVICTION. NOT THAT WE LACK THE
SUBSTANCE OF A COURAGE WHICH FEEDS CONVICTION,
IT'S MORE THAT WE REFUSE THE REQUIRED FOCUS."

Yet do we not frequently find a kinship with the underdog to the point which stirs the depths of even the most hardened among us? Is our kinship with the underdog only because we perceive him as disadvantaged or weak? No, not at all! I believe our hearts are stirred with emotion because intuitively we know with absolute certainty that what we are witnessing is a *being* simply engaged in the attempted perfection (fulfillment) of his *divine nature* and confronted by an *imposing force* that would otherwise confine or destroy him! It may even be that we see ourselves in these bridled faces and images. And so, we want, we *need* to champion these efforts and to bear witness as these events engage and taunt our spirit! And if we listen closely we will hear the very same call of that still and silent summons, "Yes, yes indeed, what if this were you! Who among these of your comrades would willingly come to your aid?" And why are we provoked in such a way? Because it's your nature, it is your design, it is your instinct to be engaged in the expressing of all that is good and noble in character. In actuality, these are the attributes which accompany and serve one well in the pursuit of our common bond, our *freedoms!*

"WE ARE TRAPPED, AS A PEOPLE, BY THE VERY SAME STRUCTURE
WHOSE SINGLE PURPOSE IS TO CONFINE YOUR AMBITION AND
KEEP YOU FROM BECOMING A THREAT TO ITS SURVIVAL. TO
POISON YOUR AMBITION SUFFICIENTLY TO KILL YOUR SPIRIT, TO
BURDEN YOU SUFFICIENTLY NOT NECESSARILY TO THE POINT OF
DEATH, BUT MOST CERTAINLY TO KEEP YOU FROM BEING ALIVE!"

WHY NOT THE GOLD/SILVER STANDARD

Precious metals as a standard for currency is, in principle, a very sound monetary ideal. The use of gold or silver has long been seen as a refined instrument of value largely due to the ethereal or intrinsic value of the mineral. Understanding the historical appreciation for this intrinsic value, one can see why the Founders insisted that gold and/or silver be used as the nation's medium of exchange. Though most Americans may not know this concept is, actually, a Constitutional mandate and one that has been persistently ignored. However to be fair, and although there was a general consensus among the framers of the Constitution as to the medium of exchange, the practice of managing the monetary policy was, arguably, not as clearly defined as perhaps it should/could have been. Thomas Jefferson, as well as many of his contemporaries and along with a few that followed, expressed much regret on this point and as history has memorialized, the form and function of a managed monetary system has been a fertile field for exploitation. With consideration to the construct of the Constitution I believe it is fair to say that the framers intended that the creation of the monetary structure would somehow, ultimately, be consistent with the design of the Constitution and the needs of commerce and most certainly NOT with the needs of the *commerce of banking.* To hold to a belief or interpretation other than this would be, on its own, contrary to the *document* itself.

Although I do see the value of a gold/silver standard, there are a few issues to be considered. Here are a few:

1. Commercial use of these metal(s) has created demand for the resource beyond that of simply being a medium of exchange. Understanding this;

2. Use of the resource creates a *market valuation* conflict as the requirement of gold or silver appropriately requires a stable (fixed) price point. Absent a stable/fixed price point,

3. There is a constant and perpetual fluctuation in currency values which domestically a nation's monetary system might manage, however for international trade purposes, the effect would be an unmanageable variable. And,

4. As we can see from observing the world market for gold as a commodity, (and like all commodities) it is subject to manipulation. I find it particularly curious that gold is often represented to be a guard or hedge against inflation even though it is not permitted to be used as a medium of currency or specie. Equally curious is the suggestion that it is a solid *hedge* in the first place in as much as it is subject to erratic swings in value which, it should be noted, is the primary signal of a false or heavily manipulated market.

Considering only these four points, one is left to resolve to a few considerations, among them being:

A. Does a sound monetary policy have to be based entirely on a gold/silver standard?

B. Is it possible to have a *two-tier (hybrid)* domestic currency? One being the government produced *fiat* (paper) currency and its second tier being a bullion supported "note" or specie? Strange as it may seem, this practice actually has existed in the past.

C. Using the *two-tier (hybrid)* system, is it manageable to have both a stable/fixed price point for gold/silver standard for coinage/notes[57]

---

57 Coinage: As a practical matter, due to the anticipated temptation for interests to melt down gold/silver coinage for commercial use, it may be more appropriate that coinage only be in the form of an alloy, much as it is now, though with equal value of silver in reserves.

and still have a free market for gold/silver as a commercially traded commodity? And lastly,

D. Does this all not lead to a fundamental and rational support for a currency/monetary policy that is largely based on the *wealth creating* engine/economy of the nation state?

I believe the answers to these questions are quite manageable and fit nicely into the alternate *hybrid* monetary policy mentioned in the previous pages. I do believe that a sound monetary policy can be both a fiat and a gold/silver standard and I believe it to be a supremely efficient system, particularly if the gold/silver backed portion of the currency is attached to a *fixed price point.* And further, that the *fiat* component is tied to economic *wealth creation,* since, after all, that wealth (that which is created by the *wealth creating engine*) is, in point of fact, what gives value to the system in the first place. In other words, if there is no economic output (*wealth creation*) then what need would one have for a medium of exchange? This is, of course, why the U.S. dollar (like many other *fiat* currencies) is effectively worthless and further, why simply printing more of it creates such economic chaos. The Federal Reserve Note represents no *productive* or *wealth backed* measure of value and the national as well as the global economy understands this. It only *presumes* to do so and having this sort of unsubstantiated value, it can also be valued at nothing[58] as it has been since its creation.

Anyone who suggests that the *Federal Reserve Note* is supported by the *wealth* of the U.S. economy clearly is living in a dream world full of illusions of idolatry. One has only to look at the total U.S. global debt,

---

58   It is important to know that when I speak of the currency's being *valued at nothing*, I support and assert this statement on a very simply premise: Net Worth=Assets-Liabilities. Review footnotes *49* and *50* and compare that with GDP less our global trade deficit, and I believe the foundation for this statement to be sufficiently supported.

the total of unfunded mandates and entitlements sanctioned by the U.S. Congress in addition to that *(budget and off-budget discretionary spending)* which is being proposed by the current as well as each of the previous eight U.S. administrations and as well, many of the 50 States, to compose sufficient support for the previous comment. Then of course, compare this to the total GDP (adjusted for our annual global trade deficit) of the U.S. and one inevitably will arrive at the same conclusion. This nation's People have been taken skydiving with an empty *bag* and rest assured that the masters have no intention of jumping with you however, know that they find solace in the comfort of knowing you will be opening an empty *bag!*

The strongest case for using gold/silver as a medium of exchange is admittedly, in the arena of international trade. This lends further support to my previous suggestion that nations should regularly settle their commerce in a combination of commodities (including gold/silver), thus being the primary reason for using the *two-tiered* approach. The U.S. Treasury would, once again, engage in the practice of minting currency and maintaining and accumulating both gold and silver reserves as well as preserving these resources specifically and exclusively for non-commercial uses. This would both insure the nation's stores of wealth produced by the system and assure that it is, in fact, an actual substance backing the "good faith and credit" of/for the very *fiat* currency it is printing. I would also suggest that there be a *constitutional statutory limit* set on the ratio of *combined currency* and *public debt* to *bullion reserves* to insure that government is never again permitted to bankrupt the People it is charged to serve.

In this way every nation, if it so chooses, will then sit confidently at the global economic table and participate on the strength of its national economic identity, each according to its economic means and accompanied by its nation's industry. The economic *dumbing down* of a nation as a means to create a global level playing field is utterly asinine, however this is precisely the logic used by the *globalist* argument. This postulate provides the further illusion of global interdependence as the reason there is no other choice. In its simplest form, the illusion appears this way:

"WE HAVE NO OTHER CHOICE BECAUSE THE ONLY CHOICES YOU HAVE ARE THE ONES I PROVIDE YOU."

This is compatible with the contemporary notion that suggests the root cause of *international terrorism* lies in the economic imbalance between nations which of course ignores the facts that all international terrorism is supported by extremely wealthy patrons. Regardless, the point being is the arrogance of this logic possesses such a degree of narrow mindedness that if one holding this position were to fall forward on a pin they would poke both eyes out!

In closing this section's commentary consider that, strangely, there continues to be a gold standard of a sort. The IMF holds the dubious distinction of being the third largest holder of gold.[59] Countries like China, Russia and the 11-nation consortium known as the European Union are also well placed in the mix. I've researched a variety of sources[60] as to the actual U.S. gold reserves however, the presentations are inconclusive which of course should come as no surprise.

---

59   Source: IMF - http://www.imf.org/external/np/exr/facts/gold.htm A very interesting website.

60   Wikipedia (http://en.wikipedia.org/wiki/Official_gold_reserves), at the time of this printing, has an interesting presentation, though I'm uncertain as to its accuracy particularly as to the placement (ranking) of China, Russia and the E.U. (Note that Germany, France and Italy's ranking of their respective holdings are separate from the E.U.).

Additionally worth considering, in my opinion, would be the value of the reserves/stores that are pledged to the Federal Reserve and/or the IMF. Which begs an answer to what may be an obvious question: If *fiat* currency is so viable, why then do central banks continue to covet the luster of gold? Why then does the upper echelon favor gold as the preferred *reserve* for its fortunes and not Federal Reserve Notes or the vaunted U.S. Treasury paper? One might wonder, then again, perhaps not.

The current practices of the IMF illustrate, in practical terms, the significance of the *four issues* I've referenced earlier in this section and though a complete discussion on these issues would be appropriate, it would be the equivalent of watching mold form. Suffice it to say, should the reader's interest warrant, further study and discourse would be valuable however, it will not alter the need to resolve the pressing issues of current monetary policy and/or its errant practices.

TO DO OR DO NOTHING

In the final analysis, on the subject of monetary policy, the outcome will be the result of focus and deliberate intention or it will be nothing at all. After all,

"IT IS VERY DIFFICULT TO FIX SOMETHING
THAT PREFERS TO REMAIN BROKEN!"

Whether one believes that the Federal Reserve brand of *monetary policy* is salvageable or that a replacement of some form is in order, in either case the following issues, at a minimum, will have to be addressed if there is any hope of preserving any resemblance to the intentions of the U.S. Constitution:

1. The public and private debt load, which has reached incomprehensible levels.
2. Predatory government spending, of all types.
3. Government's (federal and state) ability to borrow.
4. Government action and interventions in financial markets.
5. Financial/banking influences on government policy.

There are other key issues such as the economy, social/education programs, immigration, legal practices, tax and trade policy. However, I've covered these in *Volumes I* and in *Volume III* wherein we present an engaging discussion entitled "A Functional Stimulus." If you've not already done so, I strongly encourage your reading each of these *Volumes*.

Barring a focused and deliberate plan that transcends politics and vice, there will be no United States as we've known it. It will continue down the current path, gasping for breath along the way dosed with the occasional and always hollow political testimony of the "virtue and nobility of America," the anemic "We are a nation of laws" pitch and then of course, the most painful syllogism of all; *the certainty of an uncertain future* which will only be cured by *Change*. All of which will serve only to justify, anesthetize or camouflage the outcome, which will, nonetheless, be certain and assured. If you doubt the certainty of this statement, look around you, the symptoms are unmistakable and I might add as well, the current U.S. administration used this approach to great effect in a successful campaign for the highest office in the land.

In the end and regardless of intention, there is always an outcome. It is always one that is the result of focus and discipline, be it theirs or yours. Either way, someone is going to win. For me, as for many like-minded American the world over, I recommend the following approach:

"WE MUST MOVE FORWARD, DAY BY DAY, ONE FOOT IN FRONT OF THE OTHER, CLAIMING AND ASSERTING OUR RESOLVE UNTIL THE MEANS BY WHICH WE ASSURE OUR SUCCESS IS EQUAL TO THE FUTURE WHERE GOVERNMENT NO LONGER CHALLENGES FREEDOM RESOLVING ONLY TO BE ITS ADVOCATE!"

As was the case in the early 1920's, financial market manipulations are always manufactured for two purposes and two purposes only: *Control* and *profit* which are, in this instance, one and the same and most often accompanied by the advantage of a *crisis*.

The following is an example of the most common form and its perfecting cycle: Typically, the *profit cycle* begins with the financing of (or leveraging) investments through the creation of debt (example: a loan to purchase real estate). Debt-liquidity, along with the allure created by the *run* to make a *profit,* triggers price inflation. Inflation creates the illusion of profit (stocks/bonds/asset values increase), which triggers even further reckless speculation (you should be thinking the word "derivative" about now). The rapid rise or increase in the *faux-wealth* triggers yet even more speculation which then is accompanied by spending on assets that accompany excess wealth[61] (excess building of residential/commercial real estate, big homes, private aircraft, art, etc). As the euphoria, caused by the fantasy of effortless wealth, intoxicates

---

61   Which is the way it should be. You should be able to use your *excess wealth* to acquire whatever you desire. I'm suggesting in the illustration that the *excess wealth* is *faux/fake wealth,* which, as we know, is exactly what it is and the illustration and current economic climate proves it.

the system into believing that there is no consequence, the impulse-driven demand spawns more and ever creative means to do so. Once the financiers believe that the process (cycle) is no longer sustainable, it will then be time to strike and like all structures made of playing cards, it only takes the removal of one for the whole *to come a tumble'n down*. However, these processes merely set the stage for where the real advantages of *control* and *profit* are exercised. The so-called *smart money* (Fed Banks using Taxpayer Money) moves in and acquires *control*, for pennies on the dollar *(profit)* any valuable assets that the investors are *dumping* whether it be failing lenders (Countrywide), banks (IndyMac, Wachovia, Washington Mutual etc.), insurance companies (AIG), investment firms (Lehman Bros., Merrill Lynch, Bear Sterns, etc.) and yes, even automobile companies (GM and Chrysler). I refer to this process as *The Cycle of Predation*.

For those who are not among the selectively informed, the *hedge* attempt is futile; the stunned investor no longer has to worry about his retirement, he has none. The small business man, attempting to save his home also has no choice; everything must go and if he's lucky, hopefully he will have bus fare back to retrieve what he can from the dwelling that used to be his home. Welcome to *change*.

What is truly fascinating to me is that all of this is accomplished, as it was in the 1920's by creating debt secured by the government and used by the financiers to purchase the spoils. Worse – yes there is a *worse* – is the fact that there is but a minority of politicians who stand in opposition; the remainder *Stand4* the absurdity of a *Stimulus Package* and further expansion of the omnipotent entitlement program, all supported by a monetary system creating money out of nothing leveraged by debt secured by *every known thing of value*.

Closing Comments on
Value Given, Value Received

WOULD IT BE THAT I possessed the ability to sufficiently convey the importance of the topics I've presented in this *volume*. I've labored so to attempt a sturdy and forthright compilation of subjects that are, typically, only an effective sleep aid. The simplicity of these topics is such that the greatest risk lies in the inability to explain and impress upon a reader just how closely the fundamentals of economics are both a mirror and an expression of your inalienable rights. Moreover, to impress how utterly simple the money creating concepts and practices truly are and this being so, *why* and *how* they are so easily compromised! As was the case with *Simple Economics,* it truly is that *simple.*

So then, we come to the end and I eagerly await your comments and trust you will look forward to an extraordinary close in *Volume III* of the *Blind Vision Series: Valor in Prosperity.* It is the ultimate expression blending both this writing and the preceding *Volume I: We Hold These Truths* weaving all that came before into a seamless and powerful series of resolutions.

However, before leaving you for various points or functions that will inevitably consume our time between my final words herein and the first of our next visit in *Volume III,* I must ask that you ponder a few final thoughts:

Yet again: What price is freedom?

Inherent in the title, *Value Given, Value Received*, is the organic notion of *balance!* One does not just give what someone will take, nor would someone give value for some *thing* that is not given. No, in fact, you *exchange* the value or product of *your* industry for that of *another's*.

Man, by his nature, is homogenous by virtue of his species and purely divine by nature of his origins. His individuality begins at this point and follows him throughout the remainder of his life and perhaps, even beyond. For this reason, man is inseparable form the *form* and *function* of his industry and likewise, the creative engine that fuels both. For these reasons I use such terms as *organic* and *native* in the manner I do, specifically to identify the supremely unquantifiable component of *economy* that is its very life-blood. It is for this reason, primarily, *theoretical economics* fails so famously in any area other than the ethereal domain of, well, theoretical economics and why predatory concepts such as *globalism* are specious and doomed to failure. They defy the sovereign divinity of the individual and as is the case with all attempts at defying *natural law,* one can never hope to survive or succeed in an act that attempts to defy the divinity of a *sovereign individual.* Most assuredly, neither John Locke nor Thomas Jefferson, when speaking of *inalienable rights,* stumbled upon some incidental or inchoate notion; they simply exposed the truth and the undeniable fact of it!

I trust for these among many other reasons, we might finally be willing to move toward the realization of what the true nature is of the faceless shadow concealed by the curtain appropriately labeled *collectivist.* The collectivist doesn't understand *enough,* He not only wants more than *enough,* he wants to define what *it* is and employ the means necessary to conscript all you possess and require that you see to it that he has *it.*

"WE MUST SAFEGUARD ONE ANOTHER AGAINST
THE ARBITERS OF DIVISIVENESS WHO WOULD
SEPARATE US FROM OUR COMMON BOND!"

The concepts that lie behind the notion of *Value Given, Value Received* are fundamental to the self-perpetuating nature of the human *being* as they are both the defining and refining nature of God's human experiment. They are an extension of thought whose core rests in the age old reference of *Do unto others that which you would have done unto you.*

Your *individual economy* is therefore also inseparable from who you are – which is precisely why it is not severable! It can no sooner be excised from the idea that you express than can the uniqueness that supremely defines you as an expression solely unto yourself. You and you alone were endowed by your *Creator* and most certainly not by the President of the United States, the U.S. Congress, the Supreme Court or for that matter, anybody that might make such a claim.

We, that is, Americans the world over should never have to consider rendering unto Caesar that which is Caesar's; *ever!* What Caesar may have he acquired by taking and I'm of the opinion that he be presented a bill for it one that he will, I promise, sooner or later have to pay. Rome's and Caesar's *price* was their ultimate destruction. I firmly believe that the ideals espoused in the Declaration of Independence are purely and purposefully perfected statements of fact. They are both a navigational tool and our ultimate destination. They are, in fact, inevitable!

The question still remains: What price is freedom? Sooner or later we will all have to answer this question for ourselves. However, do know this: It will not be sufficient for the few to be willing to pay its price!

As you can see, we have nearly made it to the end of the present exercise though before closing the current *volume,* I desire to offer you one last pearl on loan from Omar Khayyam's *Rubaiyat:*[62]

> *"The Moving Finger writes and having writ,*
> *Moves on: nor all thy Piety nor Wit*
> *Shall lure it back to cancel half a Line,*
> *Nor all thy Tears wash out a Word of it."*

Wonderful verse best understood by considering, likely, that what Khayyam is expressing is the inviolable nature of *time, action* and *consequence.* A lesson whose accomplishment, it is fair to say, we have yet to completely understand.

What price freedom? I truly don't know, but I do know this: Whatever it may be, it is a price that will inevitably have to be paid. It may be that what is required is the fulfillment, in our time, of the *pledge* which preceded the fifty-six signatures affixed to the Declaration of Independence: "And for the support of this Declaration, with a firm reliance on the protection of Divine Providence, we mutually pledge to each other our Lives, our Fortunes, and our sacred Honor."

Trusting your judgment, I will leave the ultimate decision up to you which, by the way, is precisely as it should be.

My final offering for this effort is to present one of my most treasured expressions:

---

62   This particular *quatrain* is a favorite of my father's. Over the years we've sat and discussed a few of Khayyam's verses and their meanings. I recommend you consider doing the same with your children, they'll remember you for it!

"AN AMERICAN IS NOT ONLY THE INDIVIDUAL WHO MAY FIND ON THESE SHORES A COMPANION IN PROVIDENTIAL IDEALS MORE SO, IT IS TRULY AND ONLY THESE PROVIDENTIAL IDEALS THAT DEFINE AN AMERICAN! THESE IDEALS PULSE AND RESONATE WITH THE RHYTHM OF TRUTH IN PEOPLE OF ALL NATIONS WHOSE HEARTS BEAT WITH THE CADENCE OF BUT ONE WORD: FREEDOM! IT IS THEN NOT ONLY FOR THIS UNION TO CHAMPION SO NOBLE A CAUSE BUT FOR ALL TO ASSERT AND ASCEND TO THE IDEAL OF FREEDOM, LIBERTY AND JUSTICE! BY DOING SO, WE BANISH TYRANNY, IN ALL ITS FORMS, TO THE REGIME OF FAILURE!"

End.

A cause worth perfecting resumes in:

Volume III: Valor in Prosperity

Appendix: I

GENERAL GEORGE WASHINGTON'S SPEECH
BEFORE HIS OFFICERS AT NEWBURGH,
NEW YORK, MARCH 15, 1783:

Comments:

Various historical records indicate that the officers, who were in attendance at the event, did not immediately align themselves with the general's attributions as expressed in his speech, which follows. The army was suffering from the enduring stresses concomitant with years of battle and they were living the *realities* of their seeming estrangement from any conscious act of the inchoate American democracy.

Further, the various accounts of the event record that General Washington proceeded with his oration by beginning to read a note or letter from a congressman and after appearing to struggle with its reading, he paused and is alleged to have pulled out his glasses and said (I possess two possible versions of his comments; both are presented):

> *"Gentlemen, you must pardon me. I have grown gray*
> *in your service and now find myself growing blind."*

> *"Gentlemen, you will permit me to put on my*
> *spectacles, for I have not only grown gray but*
> *almost blind in the service of my country."*

At this point, his officers having never seen the General use glasses and perhaps, appearing so completely authentic and vulnerable, were deeply moved. Their deep respect and affection for the General was so palpable that many expressed their shame and some, it is recorded, were moved to tears. Observing their response, the General quietly left the assembly never finishing the congressman's letter. The officers placed the question of further action to a vote and to a man, suspended further action, which, in effect, deferred to the actions of the federal government.

The text of General George Washington's speech is as follows:

> *"By an anonymous summons, an attempt has been made to convene you together. How inconsistent with the rules of propriety, how unmilitary and how subversive of all order and discipline let the good sense of the army decide.*
>
> *In the moment of this summons, another anonymous production was sent into circulation, addressed more to the feelings of passions than to the reason and judgment of the army. The author of the piece is entitled to much credit for the goodness of his pen, and I could wish he had as much credit for the rectitude of his heart. For, as men, we see through different optics, and are induced by the reflecting faculties of the mind to use different means to attain the same end. The author of the address should have had more charity than to mark with suspicion the man who would recommend moderation or longer forbearance, or, in other words, who should not think as he thinks and act as he advises. But, he had another plan in view, in which candor and liberality of sentiment, regard for*

justice, and love of country have no part. And, he was right to insinuate the darkest suspicion to effect the blackest designs.

That the address is drawn with great art and is designed to answer the most insidious purposes, that it is calculated to impress the mind with an idea of premeditated injustice to the sovereign power of the United States and rouse all those resentments which must unavoidably flow from such a belief, that the secret mover of this scheme (whoever he may be) intended to take advantage of the passions while they were warmed by the recollection of past distresses without giving time for cool, deliberative thinking and that composure of mind which is so necessary to give dignity and stability to measures is rendered too obvious by the mode of conducting the business to need other proof than a reference to the preceding.

Thus much, Gentlemen, I have thought it incumbent on me to observe to you, to show upon what principles I opposed the irregular and hasty meeting which was proposed to have been held on Tuesday last, and not because I wanted a disposition to give you every opportunity, consistent with your honor and the dignity of the army, to make known your grievances. If my conduct heretofore has not evinced to you that I have been a faithful friend to the army, my declaration of it at this time would be equally unavailing and improper. But, as I was among the first who embarked in the cause of our common country, as I have never left your side one moment but when called on public duty, as I have been the constant companion and witness of your distresses and not among the last to feel and acknowledge your merits, as I have ever considered my own military reputation as inseparably connected with that of the army, as my heart has ever expanded with joy when I heard its praises and my indignation has arisen when the mouth of detraction has been opened against it, it can scarcely be supposed, at this late stage of the war, that I am indifferent to its interests.

But, how are they to be promoted? The way is plain, says the anonymous addresser. If war continues, remove into the unsettled country, there establish yourselves, and leave an ungrateful country to defend itself. But, who are they to defend? Our wives, our children, our farms, and other property which we leave behind us. Or, in this state of hostile separation, are we to take the first two (the latter cannot be removed) to perish in a wilderness with hunger, cold and nakedness? If peace takes place, never sheath your sword, says he, until you have obtained full and ample justice. This dreadful alternative, of deserting our country in the extremest hour of her distress or turning our arms against it (which is the apparent object unless Congress can be compelled into instant compliance) has something so shocking in it that humanity revolts at the idea. My God! What can this writer have in view by recommending such measures? Can he be a friend to the army? Can he be a friend to this country? Rather is he not an insidious foe, some emissary, perhaps, from New York, plotting the ruin of both by sowing the seeds of discord and separation between the civil and military powers of the continent? And, what compliment does he pay to our understandings when he recommends measures in either alternative impracticable in their nature?

But here, Gentlemen, I will drop the curtain. And, because it would be as imprudent in me to assign my reasons for this opinion as it would be insulting to your conception to suppose you stood in need of them, a moment's reflection will convince every dispassionate mind of the physical impossibility of carrying either proposal into execution.

There might, Gentlemen, be an impropriety in my taking notice in this address to you of an anonymous production, but the manner in which that performance has been introduced to the army, the effect it was intended to have, together with some other circumstances, will amply justify my observations on the tendency of that writing. With respect to the advice given by the author to suspect the man who shall recommend moderate measures and longer forbearance — I spurn it, as every man who regards that liberty and reveres that justice for which we contend undoubtedly must. For if men are to be precluded from offering their sentiments on a matter which may involve the most serious and alarming consequences that can invite the consideration of mankind, reason is of no use to us. The freedom of speech may be taken away and, dumb and silent, we may be led like sheep to the slaughter.

I cannot, in justice to my own belief and what I have great reason to conceive is the intention of Congress, conclude this address without giving it as my decided opinion that that Honorable body entertain exalted sentiments of the services of the army and, from a full conviction of its merits and sufferings, will do it complete justice. That their endeavors to discover and establish funds for this purpose have been

*unwearied and will not cease till they have succeeded, I have
no doubt. But, like all other large bodies where there is a
variety of different interests to reconcile, their deliberations
are slow. Why then should we distrust them and, in consequence of that distrust, adopt measures which may cast a
shadow over that glory which has been so justly acquired and
tarnish the reputation of an army which is celebrated through
all Europe for its fortitude and patriotism? And for what
is this done? To bring the object we seek nearer? No! Most
certainly, in my opinion, it will cast it at a greater distance.*

*For myself (and I take no merit in giving the assurance,
being induced to it from principles of gratitude, veracity
and justice), a grateful sense of the confidence you have
ever placed in me, a recollection of the cheerful assistance
and prompt obedience I have experienced from you under
every vicissitude of fortune, and the sincere affection I feel
for an army I have so long had the honor to command,
will oblige me to declare in this public and solemn manner
that in the attainment of complete justice for all your toils
and dangers and in the gratification of every wish, so far
as may be done consistently with the great duty I owe my
country and those powers we are bound to respect, you may
freely command my services to the utmost of my abilities.*

*While I give you these assurances and pledge myself in the
most unequivocal manner to exert whatever ability I am
possessed of in your favor, let me entreat you, Gentlemen, on
your part, not to take any measures which, viewed in the
calm light of reason, will lessen the dignity and sully the glory*

you have hitherto maintained. Let me request you to rely on the plighted faith of your country and place a full confidence in the purity of the intentions of Congress that, previous to dissolution as an army, they will cause all your accounts to be liquidated as directed in their resolutions which were published to you two days ago, and that they will adopt the most effectual measures in their power to render ample justice to you for your faithful and meritorious services. And, let me conjure you in the name of our common country, as you value your own sacred honor, as you respect the rights of humanity, as you regard the military and national character of America, to express your utmost horror and detestation of the man who wishes, under any specious pretenses, to overturn the liberties of our country and who wickedly attempts to open the flood-gates of civil discord and deluge our rising empire in blood.

By thus determining, and thus acting, you will pursue the plain and direct road to the attainment of your wishes. You will defeat the insidious designs of our enemies, who are compelled to resort from open force to secret artifice. You will give one more distinguished proof of unexampled patriotism and patient virtue, rising superior to the pressure of the most complicated sufferings. And you will, by the dignity of your conduct, afford for posterity to say, when speaking of the glorious example you have exhibited to mankind: "Had this day been wanting, the world had never seen the last stage of perfection to which human nature is capable of attaining."

GEORGE WASHINGTON - MARCH 15, 1783

Appendix: II

Q & A

I thought it would be a helpful companion for the material presented in *Blind Vision* to include a compilation of questions, and my accompanying responses, as they occurred over a series of months beginning in mid-2008. They appear in no particular order and though I assure you none of these was scripted, I was pleased to discover a consistency in their resolution. I truly hope you will find them interesting.

1. If you could, how would you fix the government?

I'm nearing the completion of a fabulous manuscript. It is called *Blind Vision* and it will answer this question in detail. However, for now, let me just say:

Insist that government conform to the Constitution.

2. What do you think the U.S. role should be in the world?

I think the question should be better stated as: Why should we play a role? In truth, each person should take a leadership role in the world by taking up the personal burden of self-reliance. The U.S. role, as you put it, should be to perfect the U.S. and by example, perhaps we will inspire others to do the same for themselves.

3. **How would you describe the failure of capitalism?**

Capitalism is only an ideal; it is inanimate, it is incapable of failing. If there is, as you put it, a failure, it has been only in our unwillingness to permit it to perform. We've only played with the idea – we've teased it but have never permitted the process to fully develop.

4. **Don't you think government has a role to play in the economy?**

The simplest answer is No! The partially expanded response asks this question: Where have you ever seen a successful economy where a government is involved? For any economy to be successful barriers cannot be imposed that keep it from fulfilling its promise. Sounds obvious, doesn't it? It is!

5. **In the current economic crisis, don't you think we should help people keep their homes?**

Which ones would you suggest we help? Those who can afford them or those who cannot? How can we possibly consider this? On what grounds do we think it is possible without the outcome being that one benefits at the expense of another? We should all work to create a solution in perfecting an environment where people are free to accumulate the resources allowing them to purchase the home their industry will afford them.

6. **Don't you feel there is a problem with the structure of our banking and monetary system?**

This question deserves more attention than time permits here. However, the short answer is Yes and No – it's not so much a function of design as it is the idea of *limits* and *influence*. The existing system takes on the role it presently has not from the position of *value-added* but indeed, quite the opposite. It is a form of systemic *graft*.

7. **Do you see a connection between our national monetary policy and the collapse of the financial markets which began in early 2008? What do you see as the culpability of the Bush administration for that failure?**

A great question which requires a strong answer, so let me approach it this way: Is it fair to describe an aircraft accident only from the view of the plane hitting the ground? No, of course not – that is simply the ultimate result of a series of events that occurred further up the food chain. My personal opinion is that the current crisis finds its primary cause in our monetary policy which can be directly traced back to 1913 when the Federal Reserve Bank was created and which was then whose powers were expanded by several modifications: the Community Reinvestment Act that was created during the Carter administration and then the Financial Services Modernization Act of 1999 under the Clinton administration. These are critical conflagrations only aggravated by the Bush administration's failure to address their systemic and conspicuous flaws. Lastly, I would further proffer that any suggestion that there is a connection between the Financial Markets *stability* and the potential of the U.S. Economy as being a deliberate and protracted illusion.

8. **What would be your suggestions for dealing with the debt assumed by the federal government?**

Solution? Write it off! There is no solution to the financial mess and continuing to shovel money at it will not create a cure! The systemic consequences are largely confined to the financial institutions and for this reason I believe that the impact from vaporizing select types of debt will also be confined to this segment. Yes, the progressive ideologues are correct and the system does needs to be replaced – only I differ in the approach. The most lasting solutions rest in sovereign state actions and not global state-ism. Quick and surgical movement directed at the *native economy* will stir results and soften the impact. The U.S. financial system needs to be restored to a *market-based* system and confined to functioning within it.

9. **What is your opinion on the developing discussion on instituting a "value added tax" (VAT)?**

A "VAT" amounts to nothing more than a discretionary income tax not at all unlike "sales" or "excise" types. It burdens both the *economic cycle* and the individual consumer with yet another abuse by the system seeking to find additional sources to fund its inefficiencies and excesses. Further, as is the case with most of Europe as well as other (so-called) *developed* nations, the VAT's use is an indication of a *dead* or *dying* economic system that is incapable of sustaining its government's financial demands. In every case the direct VAT concept is used (and when I say *direct* I mean as a specific "VAT" consumption tax distinguished from a *sales* or *excise* taxes), government expenditures exceed the *wealth creating capacity* of the respective nation. It becomes yet another tax upon an individual's income, which has already been excoriated multiple times before. Several years ago, I did an informal study using my own *home-town* as a tax base, and when I compiled all the taxes I paid in a given year, and this includes only those that I could specifically identify, I calculated that I actually kept only 24.8% (or just under 25 cents) of every dollar I earned. What all of these taxes do, as clearly has proven to be the case, is produce a cascading and ever multiplying effect on economic productivity. A good way of understanding this is to consider the *compounding effects of interest,* that is, interest accruing on interest that accrues – and it accrues perpetually as long as principle continues to be in place. The effects of taxation (particularly in the case of non-productive economies such as the U.S. and most European nations) upon an economic or financial cycle are identical; however, in reverse. Instead of *wealth* being created from *wealth* (as in the case of compounding of interest), *wealth* is perpetually consumed by perpetual consumption. Ultimately, as we see happening in the U.S., the system will collapse.

10. The world seems so complex and unmanageable, how is it possible for an individual to oppose or, well, maybe I should say... make a difference?

The "world," as you put it, is no more complex than it has ever been. The same conflicts, in simple terms, that occur as the result of one individual seeking advantage over another who prefers to be left alone is as old a conflict as man himself. The only difference today is that you have both the advantage and disadvantage of electronic media: the advantage that you have near instantaneous access to information and the disadvantage that whoever is providing the information can make it appear and mean whatever he or she likes. Roosevelt was doing this in the 1930's; few people actually knew he was crippled. Now, I think what you observe as "complex" is only your conscience staring at you in disgust! Throughout time there have been regular and repeated crises of conscience, which are always brought about by the aggregation and accumulation of reckless and indulgent behaviors of all kinds, which society, generally, endures. Once the reservoir of endurance is exhausted, people begin to *stir* and if we here in America are wise to the lessons of history, we will avoid the *flashpoint* that will be our ultimate destruction. Rome, being the last truly great attempt at democratic governance, had reached such a degree of hedonistic and nihilistic intoxication that it never saw the approaching signs of its own destruction. Today, we have the advantage of electronic communications which enables us to be in touch with anyone nearly at any time. The challenge today is not our being able to see the signs (which clearly are all around us) – no, the challenge today will be for folks to believe that what they are actually seeing is symptomatic of what IS actually occurring. You say you want to "make a difference?" If you truly mean this, I mean, TRULY mean this, then first: understand that what government does, not by design but by practice, is only and EVER to perfect what the government wants to do. Accordingly, everything the government says aligns itself with this ambition and thus is irretrievably skewed from being faithful to you and your rights as an individual. Second: And I know this will seem hopelessly self-serving, spread the message of The Imperfect Messenger

Foundation and its *writings*, including the soon-to-be released series *Blind Vision*.

(END)

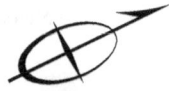

THE IMPERFECT MESSENGER™

FOUNDATION

On Point • On Purpose • In Practice

Presents:

Blind Vision

Series

VOLUME I:

We Hold These Truths...

VOLUME II:

Value Given, Value Received

VOLUME III:

Valor in Prosperity

VISIT US AT:

www.theimperfectmessenger.com

FACEBOOK:

www.theimperfectmessenger.com/facebook

TWITTER:

imprfctmsngr

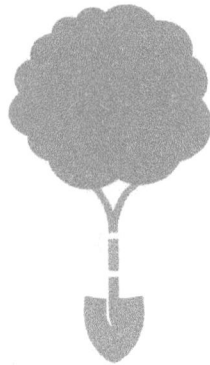

Tree**Neutral**

Advantage Media Group is proud to be a part of the Tree Neutral™ program. Tree Neutral offsets the number of trees consumed in the production and printing of this book by taking proactive steps such as planting trees in direct proportion to the number of trees used to print books. To learn more about Tree Neutral, please visit **www.treeneutral. com.** To learn more about Advantage Media Group's commitment to being a responsible steward of the environment, please visit **www. advantagefamily.com/green**

Value Given, Value Received is available in bulk quantities at special discounts for corporate, institutional, and educational purposes. To learn more about the special programs Advantage Media Group offers, please visit **www.KaizenUniversity.com** or call 1.866.775.1696.

Advantage Media Group is a leading publisher of business, motivation, and self-help authors. Do you have a manuscript or book idea that you would like to have considered for publication? Please visit **www.amgbook.com**

www.ingramcontent.com/pod-product-compliance
Lightning Source LLC
Chambersburg PA
CBHW020004290326
41935CB00007B/299